County Council

Libraries, books and more . . .

1 5 JUL 2012

2 7 AUG 2013

2 7 FEB 2015

2 1 OCT 2009

– 4 MAY 2010

1 6 FEB 2011

2 7 MAY 2012

3 1 SEP 2019

Please return/renew this item by the last due date.
Library items may also be renewed by phone or
via our website.

www.cumbria.gov.uk/libraries

Ask for a CLIC password

KNOW THE SCORE BOOKS CRICKET PUBLICATIONS

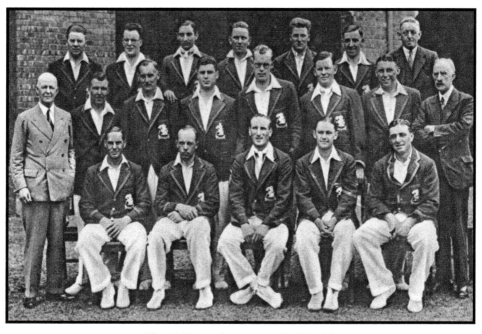

The MCC touring party of 1931/32
Back row (from left): G. Duckworth, T.B. Mitchell, Nawab of Pataudi,
M. Leyland, H. Larwood, E. Paynter, Bill Ferguson (scorer and baggage man)
Second row: Pelham Warner (co-manager), L.E.G. Ames, H. Verity, W. Voce,
W.E. Bowes, F.R. Brown, M.W. Tate, R.C.N. Palairet (co-manager)
Front row: H. Sutcliffe, R.E.S. Wyatt, D.R. Jardine, G.O. Allen,
W.R. Hammond

THE
BODYLINE
HYPOCRISY

MICHAEL ARNOLD

CONVERSATIONS WITH **HAROLD LARWOOD**

www.knowthescorebooks.com

First published in the United Kingdom
by Know The Score Books Ltd, 2009
Copyright Michael Arnold

Know The Score Books Limited
118 Alcester Road, Studley, Warwickshire, B80 7NT
01527 454482   info@knowthescorebooks.com
www.knowthescorebooks.com

A CIP catalogue record is available for this book from the British Library
ISBN: 978-1-84818-702-3

Printed and bound in Great Britain
By Lightning Source, Milton Keynes, Bedfordshire

ACKNOWLEDGEMENTS

Attempting a task such as this for the very first time is a daunting prospect and even more so when, having written what you feel is reasonably presented, the views of others come back with a range of suggestions and alternatives.

In assembling the contents I contacted David Frith, author of numerous cricket books and particularly in connection with his more recent book *Bodyline Autopsy* and I am grateful to him for having taken the time to correspond with me, a mere tyro, in an area where he is well known. However I think he would concede he became very cautious when I told him of Harold's admiration for Douglas Jardine; it was almost as though he felt he was corresponding with some heretic.

I am also grateful to Christopher Douglas, author of *Douglas Jardine - Spartan Cricketer* for sharing with me his views on certain issues. I'm sure I'm not in breach of any confidence in saying that in writing his book he too had encountered what appeared to be a conventional reluctance to concede the possibility that Jardine had been misrepresented.

When the book was in fairly basic format I was encouraged by the enthusiasm of my brother, Christopher, who said he thought it had great potential. Like me Chris is a cricket enthusiast, had lived in Australia for many years and was familiar with the cultural background in this country that coloured much of the events and reactions.

To cricket writer, Stephen Chalke, my thanks, for his help, suggestions and criticisms concerning text emphasis and style. Also my special thanks to John Young and his friends of the Hampshire Cricket Society and the Southampton Hospital Broadcasting Association for their proof readings, encouragement and suggestions; their contributions have been invaluable.

To Doctor Richard Janus of Sydney, my thanks for helping me with suggestions on the likely sickness and it's effect that caused Stan McCabe to lose form so badly.

I should acknowledge the information, reports and opinions provided by the ninety or so authors of the books to which I have referred; they are detailed in the Bibliography. A large proportion of these are no longer with us, but without their input this work would have been impossible.

To my wife, Kathy, my thanks for editing and helping me place my thoughts in a more coherent order in many areas.

Lastly, but perhaps mostly, my huge gratitude to the late Harold Larwood - gratitude for all those fascinating chats and his thoughts on so many intriguing issues. Thank you, Harold. For had it not been for you, not one word of this would ever have been written.

Michael Arnold
April 2009

CONTENTS

INTRODUCTION

TEST MATCHES BETWEEN Australia and England commenced in 1876/77 and by the time Douglas Jardine's touring MCC side landed at Freemantle in 1932 there had been 97 Test matches between the two countries and, although keenly fought, they had, for the most part, been played in a spirit of sportsmanship.

The Ashes series as a cricket trophy and term owed its origin to a mock obituary that lamented the death of English cricket and appeared in the *Sporting Times* in 1882 after Australia had beaten a full strength home team for the first time in England. The obituary added that "the body will be cremated and its ashes taken to Australia." But there was, as yet, no physical embodiment. That came the following winter when the tourists reversed the result and a group of ladies burned a stump, sealed the ashes in a small urn, and presented the urn to the England captain, who subsequently bequeathed it to the MCC. The Ashes trophy has since been permanently kept at Lord's while being fought over, tigerishly, by England and Australia.

In 1928/29 Australia had discovered Don Bradman, a young batsman of quite remarkable ability, who was to assemble some enormous scores and who literally "off his own bat" proved largely responsible for the Australian victory in the 1930 series in England. Australia as a nation was utterly confident the Don would repeat that performance in 1932/33. There seemed to be no reason why he should not - after all, if he could mount such huge scores in England, what was he going to produce on his own home soil?

However, England's style of fast bowling, which was then known as leg-theory and involved very fast, short-pitched bowling aimed directly into a batsman's midriff, was difficult for anyone to attempt to score runs from without risking losing his wicket. It was particularly effective when bowled by Harold Larwood, a Nottinghamshire fast bowler of considerable speed and unerringly consistent accuracy. It was believed that this style of bowling attack would be particularly effective in preventing Bradman from mounting any of his dominating innings and the theory was proved when his highest score of the series, in the second Test at Melbourne, proved to be only 103 runs, scored on a particularly slow pitch.

Four of the five Test Matches were won by England, the other by Australia, but as they were about to lose the third Test, the Australians complained bitterly and publicly to the MCC about the leg-theory tactics used by England, for which their press had coined the expression "body-line". Interestingly, although the leg-theory style of bowling attack had been used by England in the first two Tests, England winning the first and Australia the second, hardly a word had been said by either the Australian players or the Australian media at that time.

Previous authors have mentioned the Great Depression and the demands being made by the Bank of England as factors in the Australian reaction at the time, but that is only a part of the picture. During the 1920s, there was considerable immigration from Britain to Australia and it is probable that this influx of migration could have contributed to the perception that Australian jobs were being taken by the newly-arrived migrants. Another important factor was indeed the 1929 Wall Street Crash and ensuing depression, and this, coupled with the rapidly-falling demand for Australian exports and commodities, saw a massive downward pressure on workers' wages. It is interesting to note that although the debt commitment of both the Federal and State Governments during this time remained the same, the stagnant economy resulted in greatly reduced tax revenues and so the very real prospect of Australia defaulting on its foreign debt was of great concern to the Federal and State Governments.

Another worrying issue for Australians was that practically all of the debt was owed to the Bank of England. At its behest and to reduce the likelihood of default, the States and the Federal Government agreed to slash their spending, to cancel public works, to cut public service wages and to decrease welfare benefits, thus the crippling effects of the depression were made even worse. The average man-in-the-street would naturally only have been concerned with his ever-shrinking wage packet and not the underlying political and financial reasons, or even the implications of a national debt default. However, the newspapers kept fanning the fire of discontent and left no-one in doubt as to who was to blame for the wide-spread unemployment and social stress that would be caused by the debt default. The blame was laid squarely at the door of the Bank of England.

It should be noted that, at this time, there was far more serious unemployment in Australia than there was in Britain. The unemployment rate in Britain hit a high of 16 per cent as the depression bit, but in Australia it was nearly double that and in December 1932, right in the middle of the Ashes tour, it had reached a disturbing figure of 29 per cent. In the state of New South Wales alone it was running as high as 32per cent, whereas in the United States, the highest unemployment rate was only 25 per cent.

In these difficult times, sport was perhaps the only panacea the people had, and it is easy to see how that winter's Ashes series came to play an important role in the psyche of the Australian public, not only as a relief from the straightened financial circumstances of many families but the seemingly endless hopelessness of ever finding full-time employment. It is also easy to see how when things went wrong for the home team a knee-jerk reaction led to Australians blaming someone else for the cause of the loss. With such widespread financial heartaches and community upheaval, more hopes than usual would understandably have rested upon the seemingly invincible dominance of 'the great Australian hope' in the shape of the young Donald Bradman. His and his team's failure would bite hard at the dwindling confidence of an entire nation.

To add to the build-up of dark clouds on the political horizon, in May 1932 the then Labor Premier of New South Wales, Jack Lang, was dismissed from office by the State Governor, Air Vice-Marshall Sir Phillip Game, an Englishman, for refusing to honour interest payments on huge debts owed by a bankrupt State government to London Financial institutions. Such a move, which was constitutionally questionable, was naturally resented by all Labor voters, and so fuelled even further the existing anti-English sentiments in a large portion of the populace.

Faced with these complex scenarios, any visiting England side was going to be treading on eggshells because an English victory would be resented more than ever before.

In addition to considering comments made by other writers, some of the Australian cultural factors that perhaps influenced or were more directly responsible for the reaction, will be looked at later in the book. Comments made are intended solely as descriptions rather than criticisms and certainly not as denigration, although it is perhaps inevitable that in some quarters they may be seen as the latter.

It should also be noted that aspects, factors or issues introduced by me are not necessarily representative of Australia as a whole. They are mentioned solely because in my view, they had a bearing on the events at that time. There are, naturally, significant differences in the way Australia and England approach and play Test cricket and in their respective selection policies and in the period I am writing about, these differences probably contributed greatly to the imbroglio that subsequently erupted. Particularly useful to me in this respect has been the book *The Lucky Country* by Australian academic, philosopher and journalist, Donald Horne. It is a radical critique of Australian society and was first published to great acclaim in 1964, with an updated edition produced in 1998. I consider the book to be authoritative on and pertinent to a variety of subjects within the Australian culture that might otherwise be unknown to the casual observer.

I have also referred to Australian Professor Geoffrey Blainey's book *The Tyranny of Distance*. Published in 1966, it is a history that describes the extent to which isolation and location shaped and moulded Australia, and it has been a valuable source for background material.

The Bodyline Hypocrisy has been written after I, a Brit, have lived very happily in Australia for over twenty-five years and therefore have had the opportunity to observe at first hand the pivotal position played by sport in the country's society and the manner in which Australia tends to react and respond, particularly when defending its own. It has always puzzled my Australian-born wife that I can enjoy the spectacle of a sporting contest without being in any way concerned about which side wins. For instance I can be fascinated by an FA Cup Final without being in the slightest bit interested in the result. She cannot understand this and always feels one must back one side or the other. This is a very Australian attitude and exemplifies the feeling that the result is more important than the actual event itself.

Douglas Jardine would hardly recognise the Australia of today compared to the raw culture that exploded around him. The country has changed and developed dramatically and is now far more worldly, sophisticated and confident in itself, but even now there are instances of solipsistic sensitivity and areas where old attitudes still stubbornly linger on.

In 1932/33 there were many aspects, issues, events and influences that have previously been overlooked or ignored and their impact can be placed into perspective as the events unfold.

However the main reason for writing this book was my fortune in meeting, towards the end of his life, the great fast bowler Harold Larwood. Here was a man who had been at the centre of the storm which surrounded the Bodyline series, but later emigrated to Australia and became accepted. It is incredible to think that one of a nation's sporting villains could achieve this turnaround and I was eager to discover the thoughts of this legendary cricketer. Harold gave me that and so much more, telling me that I could print all of it, but only a respectful time after his passing. I eventually waited over ten years or so to write this book, as I had also decided to wait for Harold's wife, Lois, to pass on too. She wouldn't have wanted the Australian media hammering at her door for comment and neither would Harold have wished for that.

So the time is now, and this book is dedicated to Harold, the man who crossed the Bodyline divide.

HAROLD LARWOOD

IN THE *Famous Cricketers Series*, published by the Association of Cricketing Statisticians, Peter Wynne-Thomas says of Harold Larwood that his achievements in English first-class cricket are unequalled by any other fast bowler of the 20th century. He headed the first-class bowling averages in five seasons – 1927, 1928, 1931, 1932 and 1936. No other fast bowler can claim to have exercised such authority over his contemporaries. Indeed between 1925 and 1936 Larwood dominated the County Championship taking 1,084 wickets at an average of 15.47 and, unlike some other notable fast bowlers of his era, his energy did not burn out after two or three seasons. For more than a decade he was the most feared bowler in England and indeed the world. Australia at that time had no such talent to match his fearsome ability. Although exact comparisons are not possible, he was undoubtedly one of the fastest bowlers ever and without question one of the most accurate. After only 12 months playing County cricket for Nottinghamshire, Larwood was selected to play Test cricket for England in June 1926, and in a total of 21 Test matches between 1926 and 1933, he took 78 wickets at an average of 28.35. His most notable success against Australia came in the 1932/33 series when he took 33 wickets at an average of 19.51 in the five games.

Harold Larwood was born on 14 November 1904 in Nuncargate, a coalmining village a few miles to the northwest of Nottingham. He left school at 13 and worked in the local Co-op store for a year before becoming a pony pit-boy in the local Annesley colliery. His fast bowling exploits for Nuncargate and Annesley in the Notts Junior League attracted the attention of the County selectors and resulted in a trial for Notts in April 1923 and at

Harold Larwood in full flight.

the age of 18 he was taken on to the County ground-staff at the weekly wage of 32 shillings.

It was a late September afternoon in 1990 that I found myself knocking at the door of a modest bungalow in Leonard Avenue, Kingsford, a southern suburb of Sydney. I had come to see Harold Larwood, this legendary bowler, whose reputation for ferocious speed had not dimmed despite the passing of some sixty years. I had telephoned him earlier and asked if he would be good enough to sign my copy of his book *The Larwood Story*. He said he would be delighted, telling me to, "Come around any time."

The door was opened by Harold himself. I don't know what I imagined he would look like but facing me was a friendly, tanned, fit-looking man of approximately 5' 8" in height. His bald head was haloed by grey hair and in his distinct Nottinghamshire accent he invited me into a small front room that was crammed with cricket memorabilia. On the walls were numerous team and individual photographs of the 1932/33 tour and of other cricketing memories of England. There were a few mounted cricket balls and stumps and other cricket paraphernalia in a glass cabinet, however, in pride-of-place on the mantelpiece, was a silver ashtray inscribed:

To Harold
for The Ashes
from a grateful Skipper

We talked for about 20 minutes and then he signed my book. As I was leaving he said, "Come around any time, Mike, if you'd like to have a chat."

And so began a friendship that I shall always treasure. From that time on I did 'go round for a chat' on countless occasions, right up until a month before he died in 1995. We would sit in his small front room, surrounded by his memorabilia. Naturally, our conversations primarily centered on cricket. Harold loved to reminisce about his time in the game, the people he knew and played both with and against, and the general comparisons between then and now. Sometimes he would make me a cup of tea, and every now and again I would bring around a couple of bottles of beer, which he enjoyed. He always seemed relaxed and affable and conversation flowed easily, even if I had interrupted whatever he might have been doing.

During the course of these conversations I was amazed at the ease with which he could recall some of the minutest details of incidents that had taken place in County and Test matches during the 1920s and 30s. He spoke of his admiration for Jack Hobbs – the "best bat ever," he said – and Walter Hammond – "very good, but a bit patchy" – and his views on Hobbs versus Bradman were interesting. Hobbs, he reckoned, was the better all-round bat on any type of pitch, but he said, "Bradman seemed to be driven by having some point to prove every time he came to the crease." He couldn't explain why this was so. "It was just an impression," he said. Harold mentioned Hobbs' masterly batting on a vicious pitch at the Oval Test in 1926 and again at Melbourne on the 1928/29 tour. "I saw both those innings," he said, "and in those conditions there's no way Bradman would have survived." Hobbs, Harold thought, was a great "team man", whereas Bradman was a Bradman man, who would take little interest in batting if the pitch was difficult (Bradman's throwing away of his wicket on the turning pitch at Lords in 1934 seems to support this view). On almost any wicket, he maintained, Hobbs was the complete master and there was enormous admiration and affection for him. For Bradman there was huge admiration too, but little affection. Hobbs was popular as a person and Bradman, of course, also had massive popularity, but only as a run maker.

As Harold gradually got to know me, he opened up on the 1932/33 tour, the series during which his name became synonymous with 'bodyline'. The outstanding feature of our conversations about that tour was Harold's unwavering support for and admiration of Douglas Jardine, who, he said, was nothing like the aloof snob that he has been painted to be in many quarters. "He was actually just shy," said Harold. "Rather like an actor who had a stage image, but was a very quiet person in private – like Alec Guinness, if you like." Jardine was, said Harold, "The best captain I ever played under or ever saw. He took care of everything and, more than that, he was quite content to bear on his shoulders all the brickbats that were hurled at the English team by the Australian press and barrackers. We had the odd disagreement – you always do – but he was a great captain."

Nothing would shift him from this view. As to the Australian complaints about leg-theory, he used to chuckle and say, "You know, they said nowt about it until they'd lost the third Test." This view is confirmed by Bill Bowes, a fellow fast bowler on that tour, in his book *Express Deliveries*.

The more I talked to Harold and the more I listened to his reminiscences, the more I began to think that the conventional view of Douglas Jardine in 1932/33 was inaccurate. That, in fact, the England captain had been portrayed as a demon in order to justify subsequent events and deflect criticism away from an under-performing Australian side. A picture of a totally different person was emerging from the haughty, condescending, Australian-hating Jardine so often and populary described. In its place I was seeing a quiet, sensitive man, meticulous in his planning, caring about his team, but uncompromising in the execution of his mission. This unstinting admiration of Douglas Jardine was quite clearly genuine, for Harold appeared to be a man of transparent honesty. So it seemed obvious to me that there had to be another side to the much-maligned character of Jardine and other explanations behind the events of that tour. Also, that there may have been other factors influencing the strong Australian reaction.

I mentioned to Harold that I might write a book one day to examine the various aspects of the Test series that we had so often talked about and include in it some of the topics that had not been considered and yet were, to my mind, so important. He laughed. "Just wait till I'm gone", he said. "Then you can write what you like."

I did ask Harold if he could explain what it was about Jardine's Harlequin cap that seemed to arouse such fury and resentment amongst Australian crowds, and not just the barrackers. The Harlequin cap comprises six segments in the colours of buff, Oxford blue (i.e. a darkish blue) and maroon, and by cricketing standards the colours do not contrast dramatically nor does it really stand out like, for instance, the red and yellow of the MCC or the crimson green and white of the Free Foresters. Harold could not really offer an explanation. "It was weird sometimes," he said. "The whole place would go berserk and apparently over nothing. All Mr Jardine had to do was to make a simple change of field and this would be greeted with sarcastic comments and abusive cheers. I really don't know how he stood it all with such calm. He was quite amazing."

"And did this abuse get worse when Australia were losing?" I asked him.

"Oh, without a doubt," he said. "When Australia were doing well you could hardly hear a pin drop, other than cheers if an Australian batsman hit a boundary or if they took a wicket."

Harold always claimed the players were 100 per cent behind Jardine. Several writers have implied that there were a few members of the team who loathed Jardine and I have studied the published comments of those members who came out in print. Other than Jardine himself and Harold, a number of that team wrote books that mentioned the tour and there is, in fact, not one critical comment in any of them regarding Jardine as a personality. In fact quite the opposite. It should be emphasised that these are the published views of the players and not merely comments claimed to have been made in private and attributed to them by others some decades later without identifying the source. No captain is universally and consistently esteemed by every single member of his team and it is inevitable that there will sometimes be personalities that clash, but it is clear that support, respect and admiration certainly appear to have been there in spades for the captain, contrary to popular belief.

Jardine has been depicted in certain quarters as a strict disciplinarian. I asked Harold whether he was in fact as difficult as others seem to have suggested and his reply was, "Compared with who?" This appeared to suggest that discipline was either nothing new or was a relative thing, which in any event, it probably was and still is. I conveyed to him what others had written about Jardine and he said he could only speak of the professionals, but that there were other captains he had played under – Arthur Carr, his Notts skipper, for instance – who were also fairly authoritarian. "But," he said, "it didn't worry any of us, provided we thought the skipper knew what he was doing and we respected his judgment, which with Mr Jardine we most certainly did." This comment seems to sit precisely with Jack Hobbs' view. He wrote, 'No wonder the fellows he led were proud of Jardine.' Such an accolade would hardly have been awarded to someone who was merely a strict disciplinarian.

The point should be made too, that Douglas Jardine had already been dead over thirty years when I talked to Harold, who as I mentioned earlier, came from a humble coal-mining background and from a social order that was distinctly lower than the that of Douglas Jardine. In the early 1990s when I was speaking with him, he had no need to seek favours nor had he any reason to fear the consequences of what he said, so I feel that what he told me may be accepted as his honest views.

As to his views on leg-theory, sixty years after the tumultuous events of that tour Harold would say that he still felt it was legal, but the subsequent brouhaha had been distorted and blown out of all proportion by the press.

"That was why," he said, "you had all these young lads in Australia trying to ping the batsman. That was the way the press described it, but it was just not true and, of course," he added, "some of the pitches were so unpredictable that none of us knew how the ball would arrive at the batsman. Whether it would be shin high or up to the batsman's chest from the same spot."

Asked if he thought the furore might not have erupted at all had Australia won the series, Harold would not be drawn. "I don't know about that. I can't say." This is quite a diplomatic answer and the reason for that can be found in his acceptance in his new home to which he emigrated in the early 1950s. Harold was always very grateful for the kindness, hospitality and assistance he and his family received. They settled well and had a wide circle of friends and he did not want to upset anyone. Others have said that he was a bitter man right up to the end, but I didn't detect that at all. To me there seemed to be little in the way of sour grapes at his subsequent demonisation of Harold Larwood. To a far greater extent he seemed philosophical and reflective, to the extent that even the apology demanded of him he thought to be merely ridiculous instead of the injustice it so obviously was. This apology will be discussed later in this book.

Although I think he knew I would not attribute to him anything that might cause disquiet to any of them, I think he had a pretty good idea where my investigations would lead.

Harold Larwood died on 22 July 1995, aged 90, having once said to me that he reckoned he'd never have lived that long back home in Nottingham. Although mid-winter in Sydney is nothing like the cold damp of the English midlands in January, inclement weather is a relative thing, and Harold caught a cold that developed into pneumonia. He finally suffered a serious stroke in hospital. After a private family funeral, a Memorial Service was held on 28 July at the Anglican Church in Kingsford. A feature of the service was the playing of the Frank Sinatra recording of *My Way*. For Harold this was like a bugler playing the *Last Post*.

Although it was my various conversations with Harold Larwood that led to this book being written, the point should be made that even those conversations would never have prompted such a book if I had met Harold in England. The catalyst for the idea was essentially the fact that I was talking

IN LOVING MEMORY OF

OUR DEAR FATHER

HAROLD LARWOOD M.B.E.

14-11-1904 – 22-7-1995

REST IN PEACE

Harold Larwood's memorial plaque in the wall of the
Holy Trinity Anglican Church, Kingsford

to him about the events in 1932/33 against the backdrop of him being in and assimilated into Australia. Watching and experiencing the way this country reacts to perceived slights alongside its all-consuming obsession with sport made me think that certain issues may have contributed or even given rise to the events in 1932/33. These factors seem to have remained untouched in previous accounts of that tour.

I asked Harold about some of the issues and events described in existing accounts of the tour on which I thought some comment might be interesting. It was. Outside those Larwood interviews, as far as possible this book is based only on the published views, reports or opinions of those who took part in or watched with their own eyes the events of 1932/33. I have taken no account of alleged and unsubstantiated hearsay comments. Whilst I am not suggesting that his views should be taken as gospel, Harold's answers to the questions I raised are, in many cases, supported elsewhere.

Any questions I raise in this book or conclusions arrived at are entirely mine and although I regard them as logical and many as inevitable, they should in no way be attributed to Harold. I deliberately avoided placing him in an invidious position by seeking his support for my own interpretations and/or conclusions.

Throughout the book, unless there are significant reasons otherwise, I have used the original expression 'leg-theory' when referring to the type of bowling concerned, rather than the media-concocted 'bodyline'. However 'bodyline' has been used in the book's title – but only because that word became synonymous with the controversy that erupted.

This book has been written in memory of a lovely man whom I was lucky enough to have had the privilege of knowing and with a view to exploring issues and aspects of the 1932/33 series that have previously been over-looked. As will be seen many of these put a totally different complexion on those events.

The Author (right) and Harold Larwood share a beer on the great fast bowler's 87th birthday in 1991.

AUSTRALIA - THE CULTURE

"To appear ordinary, just like everybody else, is sometimes a
necessary condition for success in Australia."
Donald Horne, 1964

"I couldn't wait to have crack at 'em. I thought: 'Stuff that stiff
upper lip crap — let's see how stiff it is when it's split.'"
Jeff Thomson, 1986

THE SUBJECT OF the 1932/33 series is fascinating, but requires consideration in a wide historical perspective and against the local cultural background if a comprehensive understanding [of the Australian culture] is to be
attempted. Every country will have its own traditions, culture, influences,
etc, and is perfectly entitled to them, but earlier accounts appear to have
analysed these events solely in cricketing terms, when there may have been
peripheral issues and influences that had a distinct bearing on what and why
things occurred in Australia as they did.

Aspects that almost certainly influenced or perhaps were even a partial
cause of the 1932/33 fracas were certain features of the culture especially
as they affect sport. This is a factor that appears to have been overlooked
previously, but if an appraisal that takes everything into account is to be
obtained, then such matters must be brought into play. If they are not, then
we are looking at only part of the cause-and-effect picture but since there
were and still are certain influences and factors uniquely Australian, those
that probably influenced events in 1932/33 should be brought into view.

In 1932 Australia was an immature country of only some six million people and immature in the sense of being young. Federation of the various States to form the Commonwealth of Australia was only achieved in 1901. It was a fairly rugged, unsophisticated, male orientated, and almost exclusively beer drinking society, and strong beer at that. Anyone who drank wine or any other alcohol was probably regarded with suspicion. A Sydney rail network had just been established, the Sydney Harbour Bridge had recently opened, and contact with Britain was solely by ship or cable. The Melbourne Symphony Orchestra had been formed some twenty-five years earlier but it would be another fifteen years before Sydney had a similar orchestra. Transport and communications improved considerably after World War II, but in the 1950s it still cost an Australian on the average worker's wage, over three years' earnings for a return flight to Europe. Such flights now cost less than three weeks' pay, and a journey that then took several days is accomplished in 24 hours with the result that Australians are now amongst the greatest travellers in the world and Australia has become a very popular tourist destination.

However, in 1932, it was a remote outpost of the Empire and, as eminent Australian historian Russell Ward has written:

The country lived on the myth that the typical Australian was a practical man, rough and ready in his manners, a believer in the near-enough-is-good-enough maxim, and a swearing, gambling, heavy-drinking womaniser.

Myth maybe, but as with many 'myths', there was an element of fact in it. Even today, what would be regarded as common etiquette anywhere else in the world is sometimes looked at in Australia as a social affectation designed to impress those who are considered superior.

A previous Australian Labor Party Leader has recently complained that conversation today is far too polite in contrast to what might have been the traditional 'spade is a spade' vocabulary of that era. Elsewhere in this book, the language and personal abuse hurled at each other by Australian politicians in Parliament is described. It seems probable that the average barracker - if there is such a being - feels that if his political leaders in

Canberra and the State capitals can use such broadsides, then he is entitled to behave in like manner at a cricket ground. It would also help to explain the blunt language of the cable sent by the Australian Board of Control to the MCC.

'Barracking' is in theory merely vocal support for one's team, but in reality it frequently involves offensive language and shouted personal abuse. It has now abated somewhat, at least at cricket venues, but it still seems to be regarded as an Australian tradition and because of the behaviour of the rowdy crowds, Australia was one of the first Test-playing nations to be forced to ban spectators from coming onto the field during intervals in play. This is in contrast to English County cricket, where a stroll onto the field and a look at the pitch were a tradition for decades.

In March 1933 Australian barrackers were described in a letter to the *Sydney Sun* as follows:

> They consist in large part of larrikins, habitual loafers and "dead beats" or "grass-eaters" (as they are called in Australia) and irresponsible youths who will always follow the lead of rowdy seniors. They are the worst product of what has been called vicarious athleticism. They play no games themselves and therefore understand nothing of the techniques of the sports (except racing) which they spend a large part of their lives watching. Their favourite amusement, for example, is throwing paper bags full of banana skins and similar ammunition at those who stand up and obstruct their view.

In his book, *The Bodyline Controversy*, published in 1983, Laurence Le Quesne says that Australian barracking was merely the difference between what he describes as 'democracy' in Australia and cricket in England. In England he states that: 'cricket was an aristocratic recreation to which spectators were admitted on sufferance.' However elsewhere in the same book, he says that: 'being a six-days-a-week professional sport had already made cricket in England a harder and more ruthless game than its Australian equivalent.' It is difficult to see how cricket in England was nothing more than an aristocratic recreation and yet at the same time hard and ruthless. In truth, the reverse was the case. Whilst in England, as Jack Hobbs had observed, the 'play' was the thing whereas in Australia, only the result counted, non-professional or not, and cricket was frequently an extremely aggressive business and still is to this day. It was in Australia, not in England, that it was harder and more ruthless. The real difference between the two, and particularly during the 1930s, seems to have been confused.

Le Quesne also refers to what he describes as a 'demotic strain' emerging in Australian cricket in the late 19th century. This is by implication supported by Australian Professor Geoffrey Blainey in his 1964 book, *The Tyranny of Distance*. Geoffrey Blainey is one of Australia's most respected historians and authors, and he stated then:

> Ambition and the desire to raise oneself beyond one's station were considered to be vices by a majority or an influential minority of Australian men and in the equalitarian society of the 19th century, education itself was often seen as a form of snobbery.

Few other cultures would have regarded education in this manner, but it is possible that this strain in the national psyche was still evident in the early 1930s and may accordingly have played a part in events. Jardine was educated, therefore he was perhaps regarded as a snob, or so the prevailing Australian male attitude at that time may have said.

Reference was made to this unusual attitude in the Introduction to Donald Horne's book, *The Lucky Country*, and even in 1964 he wrote:

> To appear ordinary, just like everybody else, is sometimes a necessary condition for success in Australia.

A revised edition of Horne's book appeared in 1998, but his above views were unchanged.

Even today, a comment made by Australian cricket writer Jack Pollard may throw some light on the cultural attitudes towards visiting cricketers. In his book, *The Formative Years of Australian Cricket 1803-93*, published in 1990, Pollard mentions the visit of a side led by Lord Harris in 1878. This team was intended to have consisted entirely of amateurs, but a strong enough group of amateurs could not be found, and so the team included two

professionals. At that time there were many teams made up of only amateurs and therefore there was nothing remarkable in this. However, Pollard
describes the team as being 'gentlemen cricketers with public school and
university backgrounds who were used to refined and courteous behaviour.'
In view of the considerable time taken to travel by sea to Australia and the
cost involved, it might have been thought that Australian cricket authorities
would have welcomed and been hospitable to any visiting cricket team. The
fact that this team was nearly all amateurs one might have believed to be
irrelevant, because at the end of the day cricketers are surely just that,
cricketers. Pollard's use of the words 'used to refined and courteous behaviour' is interesting. The very fact that it is mentioned at all is strange. Was
polite behaviour so unreasonable or unusual in Australia, or was it regarded
as some form of affectation? The fact that Pollard's comment appeared in
a book published near the end of the 20th century surely provides an additional perspective when examining the problems faced by Douglas Jardine
some sixty years earlier, when Australia was only just emerging as a country
on the international stage. That class prejudice was behind his words seems
to be demonstrated by his specific mention of the fact that the two professionals in the team travelled second class on the ship and stayed in hotels
that were inferior to those used by the amateurs. It is possible that Pollard
did not realise that the professionals would have been paid a lump sum for
the tour and in all probability deliberately chose their accommodation in
order to keep their own company, keep their costs down, and thus make
more money for themselves.

In comparison Australians seem to admire what they term a larrikin.
The *Australian Oxford Dictionary* defines 'larrikin' as being of Australian
origin: 'a young street rowdy or hooligan', and it may seem odd that this
sort of person or behaviour is the subject of admiration. It is more likely
that the actual character admired is a mischief-maker rather than a ruffian,
and this appears to have emerged from the original convict system, where
taking the Mickey out of those in authority can be understood. It may be this
that has resulted in Australian humour being largely based on ridicule or
sending up, i.e. at someone else's expense. Comments regarded as funny in
Australia may sometimes be thought strange in England. Humour of the
genius of Spike Milligan or the harmless wit of Morecombe & Wise, Ronnie

Barker, etc is rarely found in Australia. Remarks that elsewhere might be regarded as somewhat offensive, are often thought to be humorous in Australia and, even today, it is frequently a lack of familiarity that sometimes seems to breed a reaction of some contempt. The question must be asked whether this local trait was one of the contributing factors in the anti-Jardine theme of the 1930s Australian press and the language used by the barrackers that the MCC team found so offensive. Were some of the barracker's shouted remarks thought to be humorous by Australians but offensive and crude by English standards?

This feature may be an aspect of what Professor Geoffrey Blainey referred to as 'equalitarianism' in that however unruly, at least a larrikin does not stand out from the crowd and would not commit the crime of having social aspirations and perhaps this aspect was also one of the factors drawn upon by the local press in their attacks on Jardine. If the typical Australian at that time was even roughly as mentioned earlier by Australian historian Russell Ward, or influenced by that sort of person, it would have been all too easy to play the 'equalitarian' card to whip up ferment against Jardine. It would seem to have been this attitude that gave rise to what is a uniquely Australian phenomenon: the 'Tall Poppy Syndrome', which still persists today. In Australia, a striving achiever, i.e., a Tall Poppy, defined in the Australian Oxford Dictionary as a 'vulnerably eminent person', is regarded as fair game to be cut down.

In most cultures this would seem counterproductive, and where the majority of societies now believe in equality of opportunity, the Australian requirement is for equality itself, a kind of cross-societal levelling. When they have succeeded in bringing some individual of standing to their knees, the glee of the Australian press is quite palpable. Mediocrity has triumphed over brilliance.

The Tall Poppy syndrome appears to be the almost inevitable reverse of the larrikin coin. A recent article in the *Sydney Morning Herald* described a larrikin as:

unpretentious, anti-intellectual, working-class, sport-loving, staunchly heterosexual, rough, ready and a basically decent bloke with a grin as broad as his accent.

In the local culture then, the Tall Poppy appears to be regarded as a sort of class traitor, and so any move towards a different culture or a betrayal of common origins would be viewed as someone who has let the side down. But if the description of the reason for the larrikin being admired is accurate, then this may at least partly explain why the language of some Australian politicians passes without comment and is seen in some circles as being quintessentially Australian. A display of individuality or leadership could well be met with rebuff, scoffing or ridicule and any prominent individual who falls from grace, for virtually any reason, seems to be the source of media-driven public satisfaction - a mob desire to knock someone off his perch. Perhaps the very fact of Jardine's Harlequin cricket colours was in itself seen as provocative. These colours could be worn anywhere else in the cricket world without comment, but in Australia they were the object of scorn and ridicule. Such colours marked Jardine out as being different, and in Australia being 'different', as Donald Horne wrote, was against the rules. However, strange as Le Quesne's aristocracy-versus-democracy rationale may have been, it does raise the issue of whether it was this feature within the Australian landscape that was one of the fundamental ingredients and whether, because of it, Jardine was, at the very least, as much victim as villain.

The Tall Poppy mentality may also have contributed to the derision that was poured on anyone who played football - called 'soccer' in Australia - as opposed to the revered codes of Rugby Union, Rugby League and Australian Rules. Soccer was seen to be different and therefore deserving of scorn. Even 30/40 years after the Jardine tour, Australian soccer players were still being sneered at and called "Sheilas" or "Wogs", betraying a prejudice prompted by suspicion of the new and that being the case, it doesn't require too much imagination to visualise the attitudes in the 1930s. Previous to World War II, Australia's immigration intake was almost exclusively from the UK and Ireland, and it was only after the War, and then entirely thanks to a refreshing influx of migrants from Greece, Italy, the Balkans and central Europe, that the game of soccer with its world-wide following began to take off in Australia. As late as 1969, a ticker-tape parade for the Australian soccer team was booed by large elements in the crowd with colourful epithets such as "fuckin' poofters", and "dago bastards", but incredibly as it was, most of the team was made up of names such as Warren, Corry, Ackerley, Keith, Wilkins, Watkiss, Lloyd, Westwater, Richards, etc. Hardly a 'dago' collection. Understanding what these soccer players had to put up with from their own countrymen makes it easier to imagine what visiting sporting teams have had to endure from cricket barrackers.

In the early 1930s there was a fundamental difference between Australia and England in attitudes towards authority, and this is still largely the case today. Whereas in England there was, by and large, an acceptance of traditional spheres and sources of influence and authority, in Australia those in authority were generally regarded with cynicism and/or contempt. Trade unionism was very strong in Australia at that time (even in the 21st century it still has some of the world's most militant unions), and this allegiance may have fuelled the anti-authority strain, which is another manifestation of the equalitarianism referred to by Professor Geoffrey Blainey. A large percentage of the anti-authority attitude in Australia no doubt sprung from the convict background of the early forced settlers who found themselves in a completely foreign, strange and inhospitable landscape. However, when these convicts finished their sentences and were eventually freed, they had a choice of either being expatriated back to England or they could settle in the country. If they chose to do so, in some cases they were offered generous land grants. Many chose to return to England and Ireland but a large percentage of these subsequently returned to Australia as free men and took up their entitlements, settled the land and in most cases became successful businessmen and landholders. It is easy to see that the convict background with its consequent cruelty and hardship, no doubt generated an anti-authority attitude and this is perhaps the reason that has fuelled the Tall Poppy syndrome. Today, those who can trace their background back to the convicts are considered to be among the elite, much the same as how Americans look with reverence upon descendents of their early settlers.

It may have been this aspect that Le Quesne had in mind when he stated that Australia was more democratic than England. This is something of a distortion. It was not that democracy was greater in Australia, rather that it was taking a different form and although it might be claimed that the absence of class in Australia was to be lauded, class does exist in Australia, just as anywhere else, but it manifests itself in different ways - financial envy rather than social background, balance sheets instead of blood lines.

Certainly there does exist in Australia an anti-English streak of Irish origin. Given the treatment meted out to Catholics in Ireland by absentee Protestant landlords in the 19th century and the number of Irish who had to migrate to Australia as a result, this resentment is not surprising. In the 1850s, for example, through the Donegal Relief Fund, subscriptions were raised in Sydney to finance three relief ships to bring starving peasants from Donegal out to the Colony. These people had been ejected from their land and were even being charged for the seaweed some were collecting from the seashore in an effort just to survive, and then add to that the per-ceived brutality of the Black & Tans in the early 1920s. There is in Australia a sizeable community of Irish extraction, and the bitter memories of such episodes still contribute to periodic and quite understandable railings against the English.

But let us go forward a few years to events that occurred on the Australian Test scene some time after the 1932/33 series, to events in a country that had moved forward and become far more worldly and yet where the same type of fracas was likely to arise. The country had changed considerably but the barracking element continues which gives a measure of what was experienced in the 1930s.

In 1972 English fast bowler John Snow was pelted with beer cans and bottles by a mob on 'the hill' at the Sydney Cricket Ground, and had his shirt grabbed by a drunken spectator because a lower order Australian batsman, Terry Jenner, had ducked into a short ball that hit him on the head. The English skipper, Ray Illingworth, decided to lead his team from the field, judging that he did not want to subject his players to the heated mêlée and physical danger that they were encountering at that time because England happened to be winning the game. It would have been cause for considerable concern had it occurred in England, but it was reported locally with little comment.

During the 1974/75 Ashes series, on pitches of unpredictable bounce that suited their speed, the Australian fast pair of Lillee and Thompson were causing such serious injuries to the English batsmen that Colin Cowdrey had to be flown out as a replacement. In a series which Australia won 4-1, due largely to this fearsome twosome, the seething inferno of the local crowds were chanting "kill, kill, kill!" when either of the two ran into bowl and cheering each injury inflicted. It would be interesting to see the reaction if the boot had been on the other foot. Would local writers have described this crowd as malicious in the same fashion as they described leg-theory? This was forty years after the 1932/33 series, but the same crowd reactions seemed to have persisted.

As a postscript, Cowdrey, having been rushed into the Test arena almost immediately after he arrived, thought he should introduce himself to Jeff Thomson when he went in to bat. Cowdrey offered his hand and said, "We haven't met. My name's Colin Cowdrey." Thomson brushed aside the proffered hand, saying, "Get f*****". Perhaps Thomson's rejoinder should not come as such a surprise for there are times when what would be regarded as common courtesy in England is sometimes dismissed on the cricket field here as a form of social affectation and could explain Thomson's explosive reaction.

Again, during the 1985/86 series, New Zealand fast bowler Richard Hadlee had to continually endure the barracking Australian chorus of "Hadlee is a wanker" when he was bowling. He was at the time scything his way through the Australian batting and as a result the crowd felt that he had to be put off. Hadlee was similarly effective wherever he bowled, but he never experienced any similar problems in any other country, but this could be explained by the love/hate relationship that Australians and New Zealanders have for each other. Mike Brearley was also subjected to a campaign of jeering, sneering and abuse by the cricket mobs in 1978/79. An article in the 2005 Diamond Jubilee edition of *The Journal of the Cricket Society* included a report that stated:

> Brearley was subjected to a disgraceful campaign of abuse and jeering by the crowd orchestrated by Lillee and Ian Chappell, which surely must represent the nadir of sportsmanship in cricket.

England won the series 4-1, and again it seems that the fact of an Australian defeat was sufficient provocation for the mob element to be let loose on the visiting captain. It is also possible that Brearley may have been perceived as emanating from the same social strata as Jardine and so perhaps that was the problem. Sri Lankan spinner Muttiah Muralitheran stated at one time that he would never tour Australia again because of the barracking he received every time he bowled there. This barracking recently drew comment from the renowned Australian cricket coach Tom Moody, who said that it made him ashamed that his own countrymen behaved in such a fashion.

It should be noted that Murali has been no-balled only by Australian umpires, and each time only in Australia. This is despite his action having been cleared following the most minute examination by the biomechanical departments of the Universities of Hong Kong and Western Australia. Murali was interviewed by Tony Greig on Australia's Channel 9 television, who demonstrated that his arm just does not straighten in the normal fashion, but even that was not enough. It is interesting to note that the same Australian umpires officiating elsewhere in the world while Murali was bowling said nothing. He bowls in precisely the same manner anywhere, but it is only in Australia that he has to endure this questioning of his bowling action and if this were not enough to put up with, after having been cleared by none other than Sir Donald Bradman, who said, "Clearly, Murali does not throw the ball", the then Australian Prime Minster, John Howard, a cricket enthusiast, then rubbed more salt into the wounds by stating that Murali was a "chucker"!

But to return to 1932/33, during the first Test, Bob Wyatt was fielding on the fine leg boundary, and although he had nothing to do with the bowling attack, he was pelted with half-chewed oranges, apple cores and other fruit and any other missile the crowd could lay their hands on. The point should be made that this was a Test won by England and it is interesting to note that when it came to the second Test, where Australia were the victors, there was neither missile-throwing nor crowd rowdiness.

Both Jack Hobbs and Harold Larwood, in their respective books on that tour, commented on the problem of the Australian barracker. Both made the same point that there appeared to be two types of Australians: one on the cricket ground and the other off it. Hobbs was by nature a fairly reticent character, but even he wrote:

Australians are delightful off a cricket ground, but on, most of them lose all sense of proportion. They think they are unbeatable and when defeat comes they cannot stand it.

Hobbs went on to say that some of the language used by the Australian barrackers was such that, if used in England, it would have resulted in arrest for uttering bad language. Neither the Australian press nor the authorities did anything in an attempt to curb this behaviour. Quoting once more from a member of the 1932/33 tour, in his book *My Cricketing Reminiscences*, Maurice Tate described the barracking as:

> absolutely vicious. Their batsmen had never played against any-
> thing so fast before, and they didn't like it. If I were to reproduce
> some of the specimens of the barracking our men had to put up
> with, particularly Jardine and Larwood, people at home could
> understand what it was like; but no printer would publish it.

What does emerge is that the language and behaviour of the barracker is a measure of whether Australia is winning or losing. When Australia is in the ascendant there will be little other than applause, but when the country is up against it then that seems to be when colourful expressions deterio-rate into outright abuse of the opposition and violence erupts. Cricket crowds in England are unfortunately not that clean themselves these days but, in the 1930s, they were much quieter. Australian Test cricketer Charlie Macartney, who had toured England in 1912, 1921 and 1926, commented in 1927, "It has often been a cause of wonderment to me why the crowds gen-erally in England are so quiet". Had Macartney played cricket in South Africa or New Zealand, he would probably have been equally surprised at the peaceful atmosphere, for the rowdy and abusive cricket crowd was found only in Australia.'The difference between crowd behaviour in Australia and England at that time was emphasised by *The Times* which, in 1921, stated that barracking was "entirely foreign to the true spirit of the game" and, in 1933, went so far as to say that barracking by Australian spectators had been a major contribution to the ill-feeling surrounding the bodyline controversy. This issue was carried still further by that newspaper in a 1933 editorial when it stated: "Barracking had never been allowed to get out of hand in England'. In Australia nothing was done to curb it. Another facet of the culture that may have had a bearing on Jardine and the leg-theory imbroglio was how thin-skinned Australians could sometimes be. There seemed to be, and still does, a lurking suspicion that a comment, irrespective of however innocent it might be, could be a slight aimed at Australia. Quoting Jack Hobbs once more, and stemming from that tour, he wrote 'Australians strongly resent criticism, although quite ready to hand it out to English people'. A chestnut that has grown out of this sensitivity is the myth of the 'Whingeing Pom', the theory being that all English migrants complain endlessly. There is no evidence that the English arriving in Australia as migrants made comments, and they probably were mere comments, that were any different to those that they would have made as new arrivals in Canada, New Zealand, South Africa, etc. People arriving in a new country will always comment, but such remarks are usually only observations or comparisons. However it is only in Australia that innocent remarks provoke such local resentment that they cause a phrase to be coined. Nothing even remotely like it is heard in any other Commonwealth country.

There was no contiguous country of similar culture with which to compare experiences or indeed to contradict beliefs. For example, Canada shares a vast border with the United States, and such fantasies have never emerged there and it is from isolation that resentments and perceived prejudices are more likely to be fostered, particularly when fanned by a local media that has no other country nearby to debunk such a theory. But, as with any outdated myths, there will always be those who, for one reason or another, continue to cling to them and may even find them reassuring.

It may be asked, what does any of this have to do with the events of 1932/33? Australia today is virtually unrecognisable compared with 70 years ago. It is now a highly sophisticated and world recognised influence in matters of global politics, security, industry, finance and the arts. Australian restaurants and wines are world class. The earlier problems of distance and location have all but disappeared with immediate telephone links, satellite TV, email, etc, and the work force is no longer predominantly blue collar. But many of the cultural aspects that influenced the issues of 1932/33 remain.

As the *Sydney Morning Herald* stated in September 2006:

We canonise anybody who makes it in the U.S. or Britain no matter how lowbrow the performer.

Quite simply, if this is the way Australia promotes and celebrates any Australian achieving even a degree of world standing in the 21st century, then it is easy to understand the massive pedestal on which the country had placed Don Bradman by 1932. Also, one may understand the reaction to anything that might be perceived as criticism and the resentment at anything, or anyone, who reduced Bradman's standing and threatened the massive national emotion that had been invested in him. With this sort of reaction occurring from time to time in Australia even now, it would seem that Douglas Jardine was perhaps up against a whole nation some seventy years ago when he brought an Australian icon down to earth. Even if leg-theory had not been implemented, with the demi-god Bradman being reduced to that of a mere mortal, the local media reaction was probably inevitable.

And then, as we shall see, there was the Australian obsession with sport.

AUSTRALIA AND SPORT

"In a land where sport is sacred
Where the labourer is God
You must pander to the people
Make a hero of a clod."
Henry Lawson, 1892

"For many Australians, playing or watching sport gives life one of
its principle meanings and sport to many Australians is life and
the rest a mere shadow. To many it was considered a sign of
degeneracy not to be interested in it."
Donald Horne, 1964

MANY PEOPLE, CERTAINLY in Australia, might well think the first quote
above was merely typical of Jardine's alleged condescending attitude to
Australia and Australians in general. They would be wrong. These lines were
written by one of Australia's most famous poets and short-story writers,
Henry Lawson, some forty years before the Jardine tour, when Lawson was
twenty-five years of age and living in Sydney. Lawson had an eye for the
social environment and the central position of sport in the ethos of the
nascent Australia.

Lawson was not alone in this perception, however, for at about the
same time, German philosopher Friedrich Nietzsche, paraphrasing Karl
Marx, observed:

Ever since God died sport has replaced religion as the opiate of the people.

Nietzsche was speaking in general but he might well have been refer-ring to Australia, for more than in any other country, sport is the 'opiate of the people'. Just as on a drug, Australia seems to have a dependency on sport for its identity and sense of wellbeing.

In his book, *The Tyranny of Distance*, Professor Geoffrey Blainey describes how Australia emerged in the nineteenth century as one of the most sports-crazy nations in the world. This was apparently not so much because of the climate but rather because of a society dominated by young males who, with labour shortages enabling improved working conditions, preferred greater leisure to higher wages. The lines of Henry Lawson appear to reflect that position. So too does the opinion of Donald Horne.

This constant preoccupation with sport – one might even call it an obsession – colours the Australian landscape: physical, cultural, financial, emotional and social. Considering the enormous resources devoted to sport of all sorts at Federal, State, Council and community levels, not to speak of massive commercial endorsements and advertising, almost certainly Australia spends much more on sport, per capita, than any other country in the world. The street directory for the Sydney area lists 137 golf courses, 334 tennis clubs/courts, 50 squash courts and in Sydney Harbour alone, there are 41 commercial yacht marinas; all this for a population one third that of London. If the UK, for instance, were to devote similar amounts to sport, then on a per capita basis, the cost would probably be about ten times the total now spent.

It would be a very unusual week indeed if, in any of the leading capital city papers, there were not a large front-page article over several days featuring sport of some sort. Sport is front-page news, regularly fea-tured in editorials and not just tucked away in the sports section at the back of the paper. The same goes for radio news. Almost all hourly news broadcasts include items of sports news and, in particular, any Australian success anywhere in the world. The covers of telephone direc-tories feature sport and the backs of calendars feature Olympic medal counts amongst Australian vital statistics. To say that Australia is enthusiastic about sport would be rather like saying that the Pope has an interest in religion.

However, that such a huge investment pays off is demonstrated by Australia's performance in the Olympics. Although only 52nd in the world by population and ranked 13th by GDP, Australia was placed 4th in the medal tally at the 2004 Olympics. Australian sporting success should never come as a surprise and yet, when this massive material and emotional investment produces the inevitable success, Australia tends to react as if the result was spontaneous evidence of the country's natural talent. A boy born in Melbourne has no more instinctive aptitude for sport than one born in Madrid, Manchester or Munich, but he grows up in a culture surrounded and enveloped by sport. If nothing else, peer pressure ensures that he cannot avoid being well aware of the crucial importance of sport in his environment. Moreover, even if he is not particularly successful at sport, his social image and reputation may well depend on his perceived knowledge and enthusiasm.

Such priorities and apportionment of resources must have its downside. Sydney is Australia's largest city and on average receives 50 per cent more rainfall than London. Yet, with only a third of London's population, it suffers water supply problems because nothing has been spent on increased water storage capacity for over forty years despite the population having doubled in that time. Storm waters pour out to sea and although London has recycled water for over 100 years not a drop is recycled in Sydney, which lurches from one water crisis to another. The same neglect of public utilities is true of electricity supply, with predictable demand having outstripped supply, and power cuts imposed in some areas. For a city that sees itself in global terms, Sydney's rail network is almost third world, with a number of services not even providing toilet facilities. However, millions have been poured into various sporting facilities by successive governments. One of the results of this massive investment in sport has been that the excess of sporting stadia in Sydney is such that the world-renowned Sydney Cricket Ground actually had to bid against another Sydney stadium to stage some international cricket matches.

Australia regularly refers to what it calls 'sporting heroes' or 'legends', and anyone achieving sporting success, particularly at international level, is feted almost as a demi-god. He or she is revered and consistently featured in the media, editorials, advertisements, postage stamps, etc. and is rewarded with substantial commercial endorsements.

It was essentially because of this national obsession that, with his World Series matches, Kerry Packer was in a position to pressure the Australian Cricket Board to allow his Channel 9 television station the sole rights to broadcasting Test and One Day International cricket matches. It is highly improbable that a media mogul in any other cricketing country would have been able to wield such influence.

However, Australians do not go to watch cricket as such but they mainly go to watch Australia win. If Australia doesn't win, the crowds will stay away in droves and Packer knew that irrespective of the rights or wrongs of the situation a sports-mad public would not for long tolerate a losing Test team that was shorn of its best players. So the Australian Cricket Board handed over the televising of cricket for Packer's thirty pieces of silver. It has been said that Packer was interested in the good of cricket and that may be so, but it is more likely that Packer was interested in the good of his own business empire. The fall-out in terms of higher earnings for international cricketers did not occur simply because he felt it to be deserved but came about as a natural consequence of the intense commercialisation of the game in Australia that occurred after he took control. The Packer takeover did have one beneficial outcome. More between-over television advertising can be fitted into a day's play with a 6-ball over than with an 8-ball one providing an increase of a third in advertising space. The 8-ball Australian over was therefore scrapped and Australia fell in line with the rest of the world all at the behest of Channel 9 and the extra advertising and revenue that could be generated.

Nobody who plays any game actually enjoys losing, for that would negate the whole purpose of the contest. But Australians seem to *detest* losing. As Jack Hobbs observed:

> It is entirely the result that counts in Australia, in contrast to England, where the "play", i.e., the actual performance, is just as important.

Simply enjoying the spectacle of a cricket match or the mere participation in a game seems largely foreign to certain sections of the Australian
public. This attitude seems deeply rooted in Australia and was demonstrated by Warwick Armstrong as long ago as the fifth Test at the Oval in
1921. Faced with a certain draw, Armstrong put on his change bowlers only
and then leant against the pavilion railings to read a newspaper, taking no
further interest in the game. Describing the incident in his biography of
Wilfred Rhodes, Sydney Rogerson commented:

> It was not an edifying exhibition, but what of it? Warwick
> Armstrong had throughout his long career been the uncompro-
> mising realist. His only concern was to win. The game as a spec-
> tacle was an entirely secondary consideration.

It is probably this priority of the result over the play, or the way the
game is played, that has been the reason that 'walking' – the batsman
acknowledging that he knows he has hit a ball which has resulted in a catch
– has never been accepted in Australia. Walking was for many years
regarded as a virtual obligation amongst many cricketers in England, it
being thought bad form to do otherwise. Not so in Australia, where a
batsman will always wait for the umpire's decision. Australian Test wicket-
keeper/batsman Adam Gilchrist provoked considerable debate in Australia
recently when he decided to walk. He had gone against the tide, and from
the discussion that followed his action, it seemed as though a sizeable
element felt that walking was a sign of weakness, rather than an indication
of integrity.

The national priority for sporting success is so important that it became
a Government matter when Australia's total medal tally was only five at the
1976 Montreal Olympics and it was felt to be an unacceptable national
humiliation. But there was political advantage to be had if something was
seen to be done to correct this aberration and The Australian Institute of
Sport was established by the Government, making Australia the first country
in the world outside the then Eastern Block of countries to operate such a
national institution. This Institute has now been expanded, and each State
has its own Institute of Sport. Funding is Federal and State, with substantial

commercial contributions. In Britain, by comparison, there is little Government interest or initiative in sport because there is no similar public demand for such action. If there were, and there were votes in it as there are in Australia, then British political parties would include sports funding and support as a priority in their election manifestos. As it is, until sport becomes a national issue, relatively little will be done.

However, with sport's role in the Australian national culture comes the parallel requirement for success. It could be said that the country views its position in the world through the prism of sport, and assumes sometimes that the rest of the world sees it in the same light. As a result of this occasional myopic attitude, it could be adjudged that Australia, perhaps through or because of its geographical isolation, has something to prove through sport. A classic example of this success goal is the priority for quality competition and the manner in which cricketing authorities in Australia will view an application for a new Grade team. In order to ensure this would not dilute the level of existing competition it is unlikely any such application would be approved unless an existing Grade side were to be removed. Compare this with the recent emergence of Durham as a County side in England. It might have been thought that there were already too many County teams and that too much meaningless first-class cricket was being played in England without adding to the number. Australia's population is rapidly growing and the larger States could now support two teams but that won't happen in the interests of maintaining quality of competition.

There is a saying that 'winners are grinners' or, as Ian Chappell is reputed to have said, "Winning is not the most important thing – it is the only thing". There is little point in claiming anything as quintessentially representing a country or nation unless it is accompanied by quality and victories. In the 1980s, needing an opening bat, Australia granted citizenship to South African Keppler Wessels with with a speed that must have totally dazzled him. At about the same time, Zimbabwean Graeme Hick appeared as a likely champion Test batsman for England. However, although they had rapidly snaffled Wessels for themselves, Australia then stridently demanded that Hick should serve a five-year residency period before qualifying for England. It appears to have been lost on the Australian Cricket

Board that they could maintain no credibility by admitting the one and then protesting the latter.

It may be worth considering here whether the Australian complaint about leg-theory in 1933 did not represent a similar position. This will be examined later, but is it possible that in both cases and in spite of the perceived self-interest in their protests, their annoyance at being disadvantaged was such that the remonstrations were made irrespective of their justification?

The same attitude holds true in comments made by the Australian media when South African Allan Lamb was playing for England. Ian Chappell was particularly scathing on this issue. Yet at the same time, in addition to Wessels, Australia was eagerly encouraging into its own sporting ranks international stars such as Russian boxers and pole vaulters, Fijian rugby players, Czech and Yugoslav tennis players, Bulgarian weight-lifters and so on.

Cricket participation at all levels is massive, and competition reaches abrasive levels that most cricket enthusiasts in Britain would find quite astonishing. Any cricket other than competitive Grade cricket is referred to as only 'social' cricket, and thus the type of fairly friendly annual matches between villages that exists in, say, the New Forest or the Weald of Kent are almost unknown. Virtually all sports in Australia are organised with the sole view of producing a top-class Australian team. This is in contrast to England, where playing for the pure enjoyment of participation still has a considerable following.

Junior cricket, for instance, is organised in every State on an age basis such as Under 10, Under 12, Under 14, etc, with a league for each age group and the various towns competing in these groups at an annual final. Young children learn competitive sport at a very early age and are granted facilities with seniors, a situation that would rarely occur in England. One promising young Australian golfer known to the author, playing off an adult handicap of 10 at the age of 12, was thought good enough by the club professional to play in the club's senior competition. In Australia this would not have been unusual, but his family then moved to England, where the local golf club regarded boys of his age as something of a nuisance, and the very idea of playing alongside the adults was regarded as ridiculous. Fortunately for the lad concerned, his family then moved back to Australia.

One example of the degree of passion involved in cricket in Australia occurred after a Sheffield Shield cricket final where Queensland narrowly lost to New South Wales, and Queensland fast bowler Carl Rackermann broke down and cried in the dressing room afterwards. At that time Queensland had never won the Shield but, nonetheless, it would be difficult to imagine a Botham or a Flintoff giving way to tears however great their disappointment. A similar lachrymose display came from Kim Hughes when he resigned the Australian captaincy in 1984 and again in 1985 when Australian batsman Wayne Phillips was given out caught from a ball that rebounded off David Gower's boot. There is, in Australia, a much larger gap between winning and losing than there is in England. Victory is triumph, defeat humiliation. Even as respected and measured a player/commentator as Richie Benaud has recently stated that he felt humiliated every time he lost a Test match – disappointed of course, but 'humiliated'? Why? On a similar level, it is probably true to say that no cricketing country other than Australia would have ordered an under-arm 'grubber' to be bowled to ensure the other side could not win. Yet this is what did happen in a One Day International between Australia and New Zealand. Greg Chappell was the offending Australian skipper. The likelihood of New Zealand getting the required six runs off the last ball of the match was extremely remote, but Australia could not risk even that slim possibility and especially against New Zealand. T-shirts soon appeared in New Zealand with the caption; 'Australia has an under-arm problem'.

At the commencement of England's 1978/79 tour, an Australian businessman offered $A1,000 to any Australian bowler who took the wicket of Geoff Boycott in the Test series, Boycott being thought to be the main English batting obstacle. With five Tests to play and two innings per Test, he was prepared to invest a total of $A10,000 to provide an additional incentive for Australian bowlers, as if they needed it, to perform. It is this constant preoccupation with sport and success for their country that drives the Australian persona. Donald Horne, quoted earlier, wrote:

> To stay at home or even go to the beach and sun oneself was evil when one could be playing a game or watching others play one. At schools games have been coldly organised on impelling competitive

principles. Competitive sport in Australia can still be a ruthless, quasi-military operation.

And in 1986 Patrick White, Australia's Nobel Prize winner for Literature, said:

It seems as though life itself now depends on sport, with a PM who materialises miraculously as cheer-leader at every sporting event. This would be less nauseating if it could be seen as genuinely patriotic rather than political.

But in Australia there are votes, millions of them, in sport. Describing this national fixation and non-stop preoccupation, Jack Hobbs said in 1933:

The average Australian is far more partisan and antagonistic to opponents than the average Englishman. Things they admire in their own teams are jeered at when shown by their opponents. We saw this often when there was slow play. If Woodfull stayed a long time, it was 'a great fighting innings'; if Sutcliffe or Wyatt stayed, it was 'a drab and dreary display'.

Instead of hospitality for visiting cricket teams, much of the media seems to display hostility, as if the Tourists were to be treated as threatening invaders. This difference was recognised early in 1934 by Lord Castlerosse, a regular writer for the *Sunday Express*. He wrote:

Very soon the Australian cricketers will be with us and, very naturally, I hope they will be received with every hospitality. And yet those who love cricket must be beginning to wonder whether Test Matches are in the best interests of the game.

Here in England we do not know the bitterness which these games engender, because when we are beaten we take it calmly and, after a couple of groans, forget it. In Australia however another spirit prevails. There, Test matches are not carried out as games, but with all the ferocity of war.

I have seen and met a very considerable number of our countrymen who have represented us in Australia and they all deplore
the spirit in which the Test matches are played. They say you are
popular enough if you lose, but if you win you engender an antag-
onism which is deplorable.

The Melbourne Cricket Ground has a capacity of 100,000 and is regularly filled. By comparison Lords holds only 28,000 but, even if it were the
same size as the Melbourne Cricket Ground, that capacity would rarely be
met because, despite the population of London being three times that of
Melbourne, there does not exist in England the same sporting culture that
drives Australia. 'The Ashes' as a cricket trophy is far more important to the
whole nation of Australia than it is to English cricket fans. Certainly there
is enthusiasm in England particularly amongst cricket followers but in
general, no national furore. Not so in Australia where, to a substantial
degree, the country seems to view itself through consistent Ashes success.
Samuel Canynge Caple provided an excellent description of this difference
in his 1961 book *The Ashes At Stake* when he said:

It is quite useless entering a Test series against the Australians,
down under or in this country, in the spirit of "may the best man
win and to hell with which one it is" and hoping that the Aussies
will play it your way. To an Australian cricketer there is one reason
and only one why he plays Test cricket, and that is either to retain
the "Ashes" or if by some amazing mischance Australia happen to
have lost them, win them back. And it is quite ridiculous to expect
any other approach to what may still be only a game to the average
Englishman, but to all Australians it is a challenge, which having
been accepted, means war to the knife.

Although the Ashes-winning England team was for the first time
paraded through London in 2005 this sort of celebration has been common
in Sydney for some decades where thousands of adoring fans line the streets
to cheer their heroes and demonstrate the nation's support. By contrast, an
Ashes loss almost assumes the dimension of national mourning. Little if any

consideration seems to be given to the possibility that the other side might have been the better. Naturally, there is disappointment in England when the team loses, but in Australia it seems that the reaction amounts to disgust. As an Australian sports journalist recently conceded, "Australia is triumphant in victory, but precious, thin-skinned and defensive in defeat". Rarely will the Australian media concede that their team has been beaten by a better side. It is almost as if the possibility of superiority elsewhere is unacceptable and, therefore, any defeat must be due to errors by the home side. There is no admission that they had encountered greater skill and performance. Usually some excuse or an unfair cause will be sought but, if none can be found, then the Australian side will be subjected to merciless scrutiny, with little thought given to the performance of the opposing team.

As a case in point, Jim Laker's remarkable achievement of taking 19 wickets in the Old Trafford Test of 1956 is dismissed as a freak obtained only through a pitch that had been deliberately prepared specially for him. Bill O'Reilly, then a journalist, contemptuously dismissed the result, saying the wicket was a farce, and that was why Australia had lost. This view overlooks the fact that not even the MCC could organise who would win the toss. Neither did the MCC have sufficient influence on when and if the weather would intervene. There was also the fact that in the Australian side were two spin bowlers, Benaud and Johnson, who between them took 357 Test wickets, but who could manage only 6 for 274 in the England innings at Old Trafford. They didn't bowl at the same time in the match as Laker, but Tony Lock, the arch destroyer of batting on helpful wickets, did bowl at the same time and, in fact, bowled more overs than Laker, but managed to take only one wicket.

The truth is that it can't have been the pitch - more that the 1956 Australians seemed to be mesmerised by Jim Laker. It was not just in that one Test match that Laker also took all ten Australian wickets in one innings, he did it also in the Australian's match with Surrey in an innings in which Tony Lock bowled 33 overs without success. But would there have been any complaint had Australia won?

An example of this attitude to losing teams is the treatment handed out to Test captain Herbie Collins when he returned from England in 1926,

Don Bradman: his continued success with the bat, particularly against England, was necessary for the Australian psyche. Even 70 years after his death 'Bradmania' still reigns in his homeland.

having lost the Ashes series 1-0. He was immediately removed from the captaincy both of his own club, Waverley, and that of the New South Wales State side. Moreover, the Australian press vilified him in merciless fashion. Collins, one of the very few batsmen who averaged more in Test cricket (45) than he did in first class matches (40), was so affected by this treatment that he retired from cricket, citing "ill health" as his reason. He was 38. Whether this attitude towards the losing leader also contributed to his subsequent inability to find employment is not known but, only five years later, his financial straits were so dire that he was applying to the New South Wales Cricketers' Fund for help.

The Barmy Army irritates Australians, not because of their chanting and waving, but because even if England are losing, they appear to enjoy themselves. There is nothing more frustrating to an Australian than an opponent who does not feel the same degree of pain as they do when on the receiving end of a defeat. One of the reasons for Australian sporting success is the massive gulf between winning and losing. If losing is totally anathema, then that extra yard to win will always be a constant aim. In 1964, as mentioned in the Introduction, Donald Horne published his acclaimed evaluation of Australian society, *The Lucky Country*. Horne is quoted at the beginning of this chapter, but in that book he also wrote:

> Sport has been the one national institution that has had no knockers. To play sport or watch others play, and to read and talk about it was to uphold the nation and build its character. Australia's success at competitive international sport was considered an important part of its foreign policy.
>
> Even local journalists recognise this need for victory and in a recent article lamented that 'Australians now clearly prefer a lot of villain in their sporting heroes – victory and victory alone seems to have become the Holy Grail of Australian sport.'

In purely operational terms the 2000 Sydney Olympics were unique in that a profit was made. This was very largely due to the massive public support and an enormous army of volunteers who manned just about every post and took on any job unpaid, simply for the pride of being there and being able to say that they had been involved. This generous Australian public contribution and community gesture was quite unique in the annals of the Olympic Games and would probably not be found in any other country.

In August 2006 a History Summit was held in Canberra to discuss the teaching of Australia's history. Gregory Melleuish, Associate Professor of History & Politics at the University of Wollongong (and perhaps a cricket tragic), said that one of the focuses should be the position of Don Bradman in Australian culture, as also should be the quest for sporting success. It should be pointed out that this was a History Summit, to debate how Australia's history should be taught in schools. Recent discussion concerns what questions should be posed to immigrants seeking Australian citizenship to test their knowledge of Australia and it was suggested that a knowledge of cricket should be included as one of the questions! It might of course be a little confusing for an Afghani to be asked to describe a 'Chinaman', but maybe it has not yet got that far.

The continual success of Don Bradman was necessary for the Australian psyche. Jack Fingleton recounts the following 1936 instance in his book *Cricket Crisis*:

I once saw O'Reilly playing in Sydney for the Australian team that had been unbeaten in South Africa. It was the beginning of the next Australian season and the other team was captained by Bradman. That Australian team was pardonably proud of the unbeaten record it had in South Africa, but thoughts of its record had to be cast aside when Bradman came to bat. It was Saturday morning and just prior to lunch. O'Reilly was in magnificent bowling form and had just taken several quick wickets. He was immediately taken off. He was itching to get at Bradman before he had settled down, but the afternoon crowd could not be risked.

Even 70 years after the 1932/33 tour and some years after his death, 'Bradmania' still reigns in Australia, with new books appearing regularly that explore just about every facet of his lifestyle, habits, relationships and records. One of Sydney's leading bookshops recently had eight different Bradman books on its shelves.

The postal address for the Australian Broadcasting Corporation in every State capital is P O Box 9994, the significance of this number being that the career Test batting average of Bradman was 99.94.

With this type of cult still continuing some years after Bradman's death, and over seventy years after the 1932/33 Series, it seems fairly clear that Jardine would probably have run into an indignant brick wall with any tactic that made Bradman ineffective. By the time of the 1932/33 Series, Bradman was not merely a sporting hero. Australia had canonised him and elevated him to an iconic stature.

But if sport is pivotal, then betting and beer come a close second.

BETTING AND BEER

"Give me my money, you hook-nosed hog!
Give me my money, book-making dog!
But he disappeared in a kind of fog."

Banjo Patterson. Australian Poet

"He'll drink to his queen and country
He'll drink and he'll drink again still
He'll drink 'til he falls, or the publican calls
Yes he'll drink to his fill, of the Six O'clock swill."

Australian. Anon.

IF SPORT IS the opiate of the people in Australia, gambling and betting come a close second as an additional addiction or maybe the one is the reason for the other. The poker machine had yet to make its appearance in any numbers in the early 1930s, but betting on horses, greyhounds and anything else that was 'bettable' was rife. As we shall see, the poker machine is currently the chief culprit in the gambling habit in Australia, but over $2 billion is spent each year on horses and greyhounds, with the Northern Territory recording an annual per capita figure of over $350. It was therefore only natural that betting should have played quite a significant part in the cricketing events of 1932/33.

In his book *Cricket My Destiny*, Walter Hammond says that at the beginning of the 1932/33 tour, they had heard that an enormous aggregate sum had been placed in bets against England. He also says that this affected the sharpness of the barracking when it became obvious England were going to win. The betting confidence seems perfectly logical, given Australia's performances in 1930, 1931 and 1932. Asked about this, Larwood said it was generally known that a lot of money had been laid on Australia, although he had no factual evidence, and it would have been natural for a country that was quite mad about sport and where betting was culturally endemic. However, he agreed with Hammond that the barracking became louder and louder, and the language worse and worse, as England's position became stronger and stronger.

Up until 1930, the Ashes series between England and Australia had gradually moved Australia's way. From the first Test in 1876/77 to the turn of the century, England had won 26 Tests to Australia's 20, and from then to 1912, the score was England 14 and Australia 15. From 1921 to the 1928/29 tour, with England recovering from the ravages of the First World War, results were even more in Australia's favour, being England 6 to Australia's 13. A total of 46 England victories to Australia's 48. If those statistics were not enough, then along came Bradman in 1930 with a series total of 974 runs, including scores of 131, 254, 334 and 232 at an average of 139.14. Bradman was the crucial factor in Australia's winning that Series 2 to 1. Australia was in the ascendancy and in Bradman they obviously had a clear match-winner. It was Australia's 50 Test wins to England's 47. In 1930/31, Australia beat the West Indies 4-1, Bradman again chipping in with scores of 223 and 152. However, in the following year, Australia hammered the South Africans 5-0, with Bradman accumulating 806 runs at the phenomenal average of 201.50, including scores of 226, 112, 167 and 299 not out. Consequently, Australia could quite logically look forward to a Series against England in 1932/33 when they would once again dominate by means of the run-scoring colossus of Don Bradman.

Due largely to the social factors outlined by Professor Geoffrey Blainey and with the dominance of well-paid males in the population of the emerging nation, gambling and betting has a much longer and stronger tradition in Australia than in a lot of other countries. The Totalisator, for instance, was an Australian invention. Gambling has been identified as an essential feature of Australia's popular culture and is also a thriving and profitable industry, which makes massive contributions to the revenues of

One of Australia's gambling centres, South Sydney Juniors Rugby League Club. This club has over 400 poker machines plus other forms of gambling which heavily subsidise a membership of 52,000.

the State Governments. The social cost and misery caused by this deflection and squandering of household incomes are considerable, but no Government will deny itself the tax benefits the gambling industry produces for its coffers. To demonstrate the sheer volume of betting activity, we only have to turn to the figures for a typical year, for example, 2002/2003. In just this one year, the volume of poker machine betting activity in the two States of Victoria and New South Wales exceeded $A6 billion, with a lot of this coming from people dependant on Welfare. The most recent figures for New South Wales show gambling revenue for the Sate Government to be $A7 billion. The population of these two States totals 11,000,000, so in just one year, the amount of money spent on poker machines equated to over $A500 for every man, woman and child. One rugby league club in Sydney, for instance, has over 1,200 poker machines, and just about every pub and club has gambling machines on the premises and there are over 100,000 poker machines in the State of New South Wales alone. Such is the extent of poker machine activity that Australia now boasts 20 per cent of all the world's electronic gambling machines and the highest number of such machines on a per capita basis. New South Wales has a Minister for Gaming & Racing and, for a State population of only 6,500,000 there are 75 horseracing tracks. Greater London alone would need about 100 such tracks to compete. There are now 13 casinos operating in Australia (the UK would require about forty to compare), generating a gambling income of $A2,500 million. Total gambling turnover in the country is now in excess of $A13 billion. Australia was the second country in the world, after the United States, to establish a local branch of Gamblers Anonymous in 1960 and there are now over 200 Gamblers Anonymous meetings each week throughout the country.

The extent of gambling activity in 1932 can be judged by the fact that within just three miles of the Sydney Cricket Ground there were then four horse racetracks – Randwick, Kensington, Victoria Park and Rosebery. Officially sports betting was illegal until the 1980s, but, of course, this did not stop any Australian from betting on cricket and because sports gambling was illegal, actual cricket betting statistics are hard to come by. Nonetheless, given the central position of gambling within the Australian culture, it is almost inconceivable that money, and a lot of it, was not placed on Australia for the 1932/33 series.

Although it has been maintained that cricket is unique in fostering team spirit, it is nonetheless just about the only team game where one individual can have such an overwhelming influence. A bowler can take all ten wickets with no assistance at all from the fielding team, and a batsman, provided he has someone to stay with him at the other end, can make practically all the team's runs. Bradman was a seemingly unstoppable phenomenon and, on his home wickets, there would have been every reason for the Australian punter to feel that he was on to a good thing in backing Australia for the 1932/33 Test Series. Given these factors, it seems strange that the gambling aspect and the money lost, which almost certainly would have had a very strong influence on the public and media reaction at that time, have to date been either ignored or overlooked in previous accounts of the Series. A lot of people, both cricket followers and gamblers, would have seen their hard earned and scarce wages going up in

*Bradman, betting and beer each offered Australians hope
during the Depression.*

smoke as the Series progressed and, therefore, it was perhaps only natural
that a reason had to be found for this complete reversal of the expected.
Bookmakers, too, who had offered very long odds against an England win,
would have found themselves facing a similar problem and paying out large
amounts of money.

The gambling factor may also explain why there was no protest about
leg-theory until after the third Test. Australia lost the first Test, but had
been without Bradman. However, McCabe had scored 187 not out in their
first innings, thus apparently showing that the English tactics could be

mastered. Bradman returned for the second Test, which Australia won. Although leg-theory had been used by Jardine in both the first two Tests, there was hardly a murmur. If there was indeed some other factor involved such as the amount of money in the process of being lost, then that would go a considerable way in explaining the timing of the protest as Australia began losing the third Test. However, the Australian cricket authorities could hardly mention this as a reason for their complaint and this issue may also explain why it was that a group of political and business leaders apparently approached the Australian Cricket Board to take some action after the third Test had been lost at Adelaide. The gambling lobby today carries enormous political clout and, although a majority of the population feel the social costs are serious and distressing and want to see the gambling outlets and facilities reduced, none of the state Governments have taken any action. The problem may have been smaller in scale in 1932/33 and certainly the population was smaller then, but the question should be asked whether the gambling losses were a factor that influenced the inflammatory and distorted newspaper coverage at that time.

An additional factor that may have fuelled the 1932 fire was the Depression. When this was at its height, a number of Sydney pubs and clubs turned to fruit machines to make money. These were hidden in private gambling dens, and although evading the prying eyes of the police the Australian Labor party found a way to impose a levy on these illegal takings to provide party funds. These dens did not provide extra avenues for bets on the cricket but they did further drain the already dwindling pockets of the working man. Just what the betting details were is not known, but it would not be difficult to hazard a guess that they would have ranged from the Series outcome to how many Tests would be won by each side, the number of runs and centuries to be scored by Bradman, etc. With the 1930 Ashes Series as a guide, plus the fact that against South Africa and the West Indies, Australia had won nine out of ten Tests played, it was the exciting thought that a complete whitewash of England was on the cards. The odds would have been heavily in Australia's and Bradman's favour. Equally so, the odds on an English win must have been very long.

Whatever the manner in which the bets might have been placed, by the end of the third Test, with Australia 2-1 down and only two to play, both punters and bookmakers were in serious trouble. In his book, *The Formative Years of Australian Cricket*, Australian author Jack Pollard recounts an episode in the late 19th Century when a riot erupted at the Sydney Cricket Ground. England were playing New South Wales and spectators jumped the fence and swarmed onto the pitch, demanding that an umpire's decision be reversed. In the ensuing fracas, the England captain Lord Harris was struck by spectators, and another England player had his shirt ripped off. The whole situation was caused by gamblers and bookmakers who could see their money going down the drain due to a poor decision.

A similar melée erupted during the first Test in Sydney in 1903 when Clem Hill was given run out by umpire Crockett with the umpire having to leave the ground protected by two detectives. Plum Warner described the demonstration as disgraceful and unwarranted and only a personal appeal from the Australian captain, Noble, dissuaded Warner from removing his team from the field.

However, there was probably yet another factor that influenced or even actually provoked much of the Australian reaction to the third Test and that factor would have been alcohol. To a large extent alcohol, and almost exclusively beer, is seen by the majority of the Australian male population as an essential part of the masculine identity. Drinking beer with his mates is what a bloke does. Reference was made earlier to the fact that in the early 1930s anyone who drank wine would have been regarded with some suspicion and according to a recent article in *The Australian*, asking for a glass of wine with a meal could have provoke the rejoinder, "What are you, some kind of poof?" or a similar rejoinder such as, "The dining room is for eating, and the bar is for drinking". With attitudes of this sort in the background, it is perhaps easier to see that Douglas Jardine would have been a relatively simple target for the press and the ridicule of the barrackers. Although male attitudes towards women have improved considerably from the time when a woman was seen as little more than an inconvenient necessity, the male feelings towards his beer and his mates have not changed that much. One only has to witness the increase in the volume of behavioural problems as alcohol takes hold at cricket matches and other similar sporting venues for this to be demonstrated today, but in the early 1930s when there was little else except betting and beer as social outlets

GOODBYE ›› MEN-ONLY BARS

Men shoulder to shoulder in the public bar, downing brew after brew under a thick nebula of bluish smoke; women partitioned off in the "ladies' lounge", chatting, shelling peas, sewing, shouting shandies. For the first half of the 20th century, this was the face of pub life across Australia. In testosterone-charged pubs with no ladies' lounges (such as the one pictured), women dutifully waited in the car or huddled near the saloon doors as their husbands or boyfriends ferried drinks outside. In the late 1960s, the law changed, women were allowed to be served in public bars and the walls separating the ladies' lounges came tumbling down.   *Greg Callaghan*

*In the 1930s Australian bars were very much the preserve of the male,
as this recent article explains.*

for the Australian male it proved a potent concoction - particularly when the national cricketing icon and the national cricket team were on the losing end!

In his book *The Tyranny of Distance* author Geoffrey Blainey describes Australia as a society that was very much male-dominated until the 20th century; a society where, due to the dearth of women, men had only themselves to support, and consequently, much of this personal affluence was spent on alcohol and gambling. The incidence of drunkenness in the late 19th century was high. This problem continued into the 20th century, culminating in a massive riot fuelled by alcohol at an army barracks in Sydney in 1916. This appears to have been the final straw and consequently prompted the Government, with the active lobbying of the churches, to introduce a 6pm closing time for all pubs which became known as the '6 o'clock swill'. This was another uniquely Australian phenomenon, and it lasted until 1954. With only an hour available for drinking in the pubs after the working day was finished, it became a common practice for men to down as many beers as possible in the short time allowed by the law. It was estimated that 90 per cent of all alcohol drunk was consumed between 5pm and 6pm. This was a period of drinking frenzy and pub bars were designed to cater for it. Bar faces and walls were tiled, and the floors were linoleum for easy cleaning while some patrons strapped themselves to the bar rail to maintain their position and posture! And this happened five days a week throughout Australia! The *Sydney Morning Herald* described it recently as: 'The ritual filling-of-the-jars, the 5 o'clock rush-to-inebriate, the synchronised public vomiting'.

In the 1930s pubs in Australia were fundamentally male preserves and, for the main part, simply places to get drunk. The men corralled themselves in one area, whilst any women were dispatched to a separate part of the building for their sherry or port and lemons. In fact, only a brave woman would drink in a pub on her own, even if the rare ladies' lounge did exist. All pubs in Australia were in effect what would have been seen as public bars in England. Whether this was due to mere egalitarianism or simple function is difficult to decipher, but perhaps the attitude was: 'if it works as it is, then why spend money to make it more attractive?'

Even 20 years later little had changed and an English teacher, out in Australia on a short contract in 1953, noted:

> the pubs were frequented only by men and from the little I saw as I walked past they looked like men's toilets, white tiles from floor to ceiling. You didn't want to walk past if it was coming up to 6 pm as that was when they closed and the Aussie men in there tried to drink as much as possible before that time. Many could be seen lying dead drunk in the gutter.

Donald Horne noted in his book:

> For ordinary people it was a brutal pleasure – jostled in austerely equipped bars, dazed by the bedlam, gulping beer down and perhaps later spewing it up.

Beer was the preferred drink of the Australian male and to a far greater extent than in England. It was seen as quintessentially working-class and masculine, 'the sweating, beer-swilling Aussie bloke,' as the *Sydney Morning* Herald recently put it and 'the hard-working, true-blue, beer-drinking Aussie male'. Time was when an Australian working man would spend as much on beer in a week as he did on his mortgage and be proud of it. A light beer would only be risked if no one was watching. Sections in cricket grounds such as the old Hill at the Sydney Cricket Ground were areas for the massive consumption of beer, with the crowd behaviour becoming increasingly boorish, loud and offensive as the day's play wore on and a combination of sun, heat and alcohol took its toll. To some extent this continues today.

In 1932/33, Australian cricket crowds were essentially male and, with the potentially dangerous combination of male 'mateship' coupled with beer and betting, the increasingly aggressive and antagonistic behaviour falls into perspective in a series that unexpectedly drifted away from Australia. During this time, the consumption of beer together with betting, would easily have fuelled cricket crowd antagonisms and when you add to this the no doubt biased distortions and inventions of a local press coupled with serious unemployment blamed partly on England, it is not difficult to see that the slightest spark, or incident, would have fired this tinder-dry situation. Even today, this landscape is largely unchanged. Early in 2004, State and Test cricketer David Hookes was killed at the age of 48 outside a Melbourne pub in a drunken brawl for which he was partially responsible. Although he played in only 23 Tests, with a modest batting average of 34, his death was greeted as a national tragedy, almost as though a demi-god had passed on. The *Sydney Morning Herald* described him as an immature, extroverted, egocentric character, whose language was frequently crude, who drank too much, and whose attitude towards women was stone age. Yet he seems to have been admired as a typical Australian larrikin. These factors, plus cricket and beer, combined to create a press hero. Such was the reaction that the house of the security guard involved in the fracas was fire-bombed and the hotel itself was subjected to physical attack and damage. It was a quite astonishing response to the death of someone who was hardly a role model and who, in any event, had largely brought his demise on himself. But to some he was a cricketer, had played for Australia, and so must have been a 'hero'! A later newspaper article, examining his death, quoted reports that drunkenness is not only tolerated but is actually celebrated. Moreover, punch-ups outside pubs were all a part of what was proudly described as 'Australian drinking culture', a culture the National Drug and Alcohol Research Centre has recently described as 'revolting'. It may be said that England is now drifting in the same direction, but Australia got there first and a long time ago.

With a lost Series, some reaction might have occurred anyway, but leg-theory, the relative failure of the national cricketing icon, lost jobs, lost wagers, alcohol and colourful exaggerations in the press ensured that all these disappointments grew into a sort of rage. A target to blame this rage on had to be found, and that target seems to have been Douglas Jardine.

And who better to fan this resentment than the press?

THE AUSTRALIAN PRESS

"The Australian Press – publish and be damned."

Lee Kuan Yew, Singapore Senior Statesman

"The Press Gang, during the heat of the contest, boasted a
fighting force of 30 strong. Some knew little about modern
cricket tactics, but knew all about the collecting of news."

Arthur Mailey, 1933

IN ANY COUNTRY the Press can play a crucial role in moulding public
opinion. In the early 1930s, other than the wireless, which was still in
relative infancy, the printed form was the only source of news, views and
opinions. This was true of any country at that time, but was perhaps particularly so for a nation like Australia where a population of only six million
occupied a land mass the size of the United States. Vast distances meant
that only those within daily travelling reach of the coastal fringe cities
could actually see for themselves the cricketing developments as they
unfolded. Everyone else was almost entirely reliant upon what they read in
their newspapers and as sport was a national obsession, the local Press had
a ready-made and avid market for almost anything they cared to print.

The Australian Press can be one of the most inflammatory and personally vicious in the world. Although mainly broadsheet in size the style and
quality are largely tabloid. Describing the Australian Press in his book *The
Lucky Country* Donald Horne wrote:

There are no 'quality' daily or Sunday newspapers of the standard of those in London, New York or Western Europe, and no journals of record and opinion as independent, as strongly established, as well-staffed and as well provided with contributors as the 'quality' periodicals of Britain and Western Europe.

The question may well be asked: Well, what about the British tabloids? Their excesses are well documented but in Britain there are also the balancing factors of more measured nationals such as the *Daily Telegraph*, *The Times* and the *Guardian*. There is no equivalent restraining influence in Australia. That is not to say that there are no mature, responsible, balanced and experienced Australian journalists, there certainly are, but the overall tenor of the local press is broadly as described. Australia's largest city, Sydney, for instance, is served by only two newspapers, both concentrating on sensationalist local news and since this is the position in the 21st century, it is not difficult to imagine the part played by the local Press in 1932/33 in whipping up sentiment that was a major factor in public and cricket crowd reactions. As far as the Australian Cricket Board was concerned this may well have been quite welcome because the fictions and exaggerations helped to create a controversy that would have swelled the cricketing crowds even further and provided a boost to the ACB coffers. On top of that, the Board, being made up almost entirely of businessmen, may well have contained members with Press interests.

A number of the English team who later wrote books about the tour or made reference to it commented on the role played by the Australian Press in 1932/33 in whipping up public feelings through false reporting, distortion and fabrication, and these must have had an effect. Writing of that tour in his book *The Fight of the Ashes 1932-3* Jack Hobbs said:

Great campaigning by the lower sections of the Press helped to mould opinion against England. One yellow-Press heading I remember was 'England expects every man to bowl 'em out or lay 'em out'. Leg-theory became a first class news stunt quite out-classing the mere play.

Jack Hobbs, recently retired in 1933, mild-mannered and hugely respected, described the Australian press as 'yellow' in his book about the Bodyline tour.

Hobbs was a very mild-tempered man, not given to colourful hyperbole or exaggeration and therefore it would not be unreasonable to take his description of a section of the Press as 'yellow' as fairly strong criticism of irresponsible and inflammatory journalism.

The first press invention appeared in Perth, just as the tour had started. According to Harold Larwood, a reporter for the Sydney Sun, Claude Corbett, asked Jardine to help him get a scoop for his paper, an afternoon tabloid, by giving him the MCC team selections each morning. Larwood says that Jardine frowned for a moment at the request, then with a wry smile said, "What damned rot! We didn't come here to provide scoops for yours or any other bally paper." Corbett then rushed off a piece for his paper accusing Jardine of being very rude and totally un-cooperative. When discussing this trivial incident with Harold Larwood, he said that Jardine's real reason was nothing more than tactical in that he was not going to assist the opposition by telling them what his team was going to be some time before the actual match. Larwood said that he did not for one moment think it was intended as a snub, but he agreed with what Walter Hammond had said: "they had it waiting for him before he set foot in Australia at all" and therefore every opportunity was going to be grabbed by the press for all it was worth.

The MCC were 20 minutes late in taking the field for the first match against Western Australia and once more this was reported by Corbett as a calculated insult, saying that Jardine had deliberately kept the Australian crowd waiting simply because he had gone shopping. Asked about this, Harold said he was in the team for the first match but he couldn't recall exactly what the reason was, probably a combination of factors but it certainly wasn't because of some silly shopping expedition. However, once more the press were concocting their own versions of events. When the team arrived in Adelaide Jardine asked to see Corbett, in the presence of Plum Warner to complain about his distorted stories. Jardine told Corbett he was about to reply to a letter he had received from an English friend living in Australia and in view of what he had said he asked Corbett if he wished to add any comment of his own. This episode had already appeared in print but not the full details of the language used by Corbett. Talking it over with Harold Larwood later, he said that the actual words used by Corbett then were:

Yes, Mr Jardine. There is something you can add. You can tell him from me that my comment is this: You can go and get fucked.

It would have been unthinkable for an English reporter to have used such language to a visiting captain but faced with that style of retort it is perhaps not surprising that from that moment on Jardine felt it safer to keep the Australian press at arms length. Was this, though, a case of the sensitivity to criticism observed by Jack Hobbs? Was Corbett's original reaction just another example of an ordinary comment being mistakenly perceived as some sort of aspersion?

Such had been the consistent Press exaggeration that, according to Australian authors Coleman and Edward in their book *Eddie Gilbert* one Queensland newspaper wrote, inter alia:

The all-important topic of the day is not the war between China and Japan, the disappearance of Hinkler [an Australian aviator],

Smithy's flight across the Tasman [another aviator], or even the Depression, it is the overwhelming public opinion against England's shock tactics.

Those were the days before television and television replays and therefore what appeared in the newspapers was the only interpretation, description and source of information for the general public. The man in the street reading his local paper had no way of knowing whether what was published was accurate or truthful and would quite naturally have taken anything printed as gospel.

Many of these distortions or inventions were aimed at Jardine himself. In his book *My Cricket Reminiscences* Maurice Tate speaks of a Press report that he and Jardine had been involved in such a vicious argument that Tate had thrown a glass of beer at Jardine. This was utter nonsense. As Tate said in his own book on the Bodyline series, had he done anything so outrageous he would have been packed off on the next boat home, and quite rightly so. The English team congratulated Tate on his accuracy because at the time of the alleged incident Jardine and Tate were sixty miles apart. The Press also alleged that Tate had bruised knuckles because he and Jardine had come to blows on the staircase of an Adelaide hotel over Tate's omission from the Test sides. Tate was disappointed at not being selected, and quite naturally so, but anyone who knew Maurice Tate – and clearly the Australian Press didn't and the public couldn't – would have known that such a reaction or behaviour would have been totally out of character. Tate went on to say:

> We were all pleased the Tests were over. There has never been a series that occasioned so much bad blood, much of it I am sure, stirred up by the Australian Press and aided by the failure of their idol, Don Bradman, whom they expected to get a hundred every innings.

The Australian media was trying to sow dissension in the MCC ranks and also to show that such dissension existed. The problem faced by the MCC team was that there was no means by which to demonstrate that these inventions were just that – inventions – and therefore such fictions only added, as intended, to the anti-Jardine fuel being stoked up by the local Press. Statements could be made to the Press in response, but these would only be written off as a predictable management contrivance.

When discussing this with Harold Larwood, his comment was that although Tate might have been disappointed, having him as a back-up did make some sense. "In Australia's summer climate you wouldn't want your front-line fast bowlers having to play in every match," he said. "And having Maurice available meant they could have rest from time to time". Tate was then nearly 37 and couldn't have been expected to be as sharp as he was eight years earlier when he had taken 38 Test wickets in the 1924/25 series. In fact, outside the Test matches he bowled 97 overs during the tour, compared with Larwood's 55 and Allen's 80, so he was clearly of value to the team. However, even in the 1928/29 Series, Tate's 17 Test wickets had only been achieved at the relatively high average of 40.7, and so four years later a younger man might have been a better longer-term choice. In 1946/47 a similar fate was to befall Bill Voce, whose Test performance then was 0 for 160, and also Alec Bedser in 1954/55. They were both at those points about the same age as Tate. Although he had taken 39 wickets in the 1953 Ashes series, Bedser played in only the first Test under Hutton in that 54/5 series, who then relied on the pure speed of the younger Tyson and Statham.

Other local Press comment included statements such as:

A touring side from that country has never before been so much at war with itself, and Jardine's culpable lack of popularity as a leader must be the subject of some enquiry.

The team presentation to Jardine must have been something of an embarrassment to the journalist who thought up that one or perhaps it was just swept under the carpet as an inconvenience. In fact, the team presentation does not appear to have been reported at all in the Australian Press, at least the author has been unable to find any comment. Harold Larwood said that the consistent and widespread Australian Press fiction of dissension amongst the English team reached such a level that the night before the Adelaide Test, a team meeting was held at their hotel. The Press inventions had been clearly designed to create discord in the English ranks, persuading the MCC management to put a stop to them and at last issue a statement clarifying the true position of total team loyalty behind Jardine. However, this not surprisingly, was not enough for one paper, which still said: 'It can be stated definitely that some members of the visiting team are in conflict with the official management notification'. Nothing, it would appear, was going to put a stop to the Australian Press' attitude, so therefore the wisest course was probably just to keep quiet rather than respond to each ensuing allegation with a denial which would then be portrayed by the Press as yet another lie.

Gubby Allen's letters are referred to elsewhere, and some of his descriptions of his own colleagues are derogatory, but to be fair to the man one must assume that there were aspects reported to his parents that were reasonably accurate. Shortly before the third Test, he wrote of the Australian press:

The newspapers and general public in this country, though they have all been exceedingly nice to me, are simply dreadful and far worse than in England. They never leave Douglas Jardine alone for a minute and they publish the most unfounded statements which are extremely libellous but, of course, one can do nothing about it.

This account from Allen seems to bear out the comments about the Press made by Tate, Hobbs, Mailey and Larwood.

In spite of a succession of Ashes wins by Australia in England, even the English tabloids never stooped to such levels or contrived such inventions in an attempt to upset the opposition but it seems to be a measure of the unfortunate lengths to which the Press will go in Australia. However, the people of Sydney, Melbourne, Adelaide or Brisbane would not have known this. It was all grist to the inventive mill of the media but would they have troubled had Australia been winning? The Nawab of Pataudi played in only the first two Tests in 1932/33. Once more, the local media produced their own invention and reported that the reason he was dropped was solely because he had declined to move into the leg-trap, as requested by Jardine during the second Test. The same allegation was made by Bill O'Reilly in his foreword to Philip Derriman's 1984 book *Bodyline*, where he says that Pataudi was dropped for 'disciplinary reasons'. Of course, such an interpretation makes good copy, but it is some way off the mark. Much has been made in Australia of the comment made by Jardine when Pataudi said he would rather not move into the leg-trap when he said, "I see his Highness is a conscientious objector", but as Harold Larwood observed, Jardine had a very dry sense of humour and he thought there was nothing malicious in this remark.

In the first Test, Pataudi had made a century, 102, but it took six hours to achieve and it was an innings reported by one London newspaper as probably the worst century in Test match history. In the second Test, he made just 15 and 5, falling on both occasions to the spinners. The left-handed Paynter was brought in for the next three Tests, mainly to counter the leg-spin of O'Reilly. In three innings, and almost entirely due to the one century, Pataudi ended the series with an average of 40.66 and Paynter had a series average of 61.33. In career figures, Pataudi played in only six Tests, including three matches for India, and ended with 199 runs at an average of just 19.9. Paynter, on the other hand, played in 20 Test matches, scoring 1,540 runs at 59.23. Only one English batsman has a higher average and that is Herbert Sutcliffe with 60.73. When talking to Harold Larwood about the Australian contrivance he said that although Pataudi was a good bat in County cricket he reckoned he was not quite up to Test standard and that everyone in the team understood the real reason behind Paynter's selection in his stead. Pataudi's Test statistics seem to bear out this opinion and the change appears to have been vindicated. There have been other cases of batsmen who thrived at County level but never seemed to be able to make it in the Test arena. Don Kenyon, for instance, was a consistently heavy scorer in the County Championship, with a total of over 37,000 runs and 74 centuries, and yet, in 8 Test opportunities, his batting average was only 12. The same, more recently, has been the experience of Graeme Hick, scorer (at the time of writing) of 136 centuries, but with a poor Test average of only 31.

Regarding the Australian Press' efforts to portray Jardine as unpopular, Harold Larwood said they had heard of reports that the team didn't like Jardine's insistence that fielders always had to return the ball to the wicket keeper. First of all, he said, it wasn't a rigid requirement and secondly as a general rule he felt it was a sensible idea anyway and he recalled the team felt the same way. Larwood's memory appeared to be confirmed some six years after his death by Jack Pollard's book *The Bradman Years* which was published in 2001. In that book Pollard makes the same allegations about both Pataudi and fielding. Referring to Jack Hobbs again, he commented:

I have a feeling that if Larwood and leg-theory had been Australian, the crowds there would have laughed and applauded had our men been discomforted.

He says in his book on the series *The Fight for the Ashes 1932-33* that the barracking was fostered by a considerable section of the Press, which seemed to attack visiting teams more and more each tour and that it had assumed large and highly unpleasant proportions. Also, he said, and this is a point that did not appear to sink in with the Australian authorities, it was not in the interests of Australia that sensational news about their barrackers should be spread around the world.

Arthur Mailey, himself an Australian journalist and Test bowler, referred to the local Press as 'The Press Gang'. He wrote of the craving for news becoming so intense that the Press Gang moved off in mass formation to the smaller country skirmishes, took up positions, arranged observation posts and went 50-50 with whatever booty was captured. He reported how the Press Gang 'gloated' over the Chairman of Ballarat who in a luncheon speech welcoming the MCC team blurted out something about the impropriety of the bodyline attack and that even in the sleepy town of Toowoomba there occurred a Press rumpus over "filthy lucre" when all that was involved was some minor accounting discrepancy between MCC and the local authorities. Mailey said the Press Gang boasted a fighting force of about 30. Some knew little about modern cricket tactics but all knew about the collecting of news. The intensity of the campaign was such that during the third Test at Adelaide 130,000 words were wired and cabled to all parts of the world. In those days that was a considerable volume.

To such lengths did the Australian press go that Larwood said he knew of a newspaper having reported Richardson as saying that even if he took guard a foot outside the leg stump Larwood still fired the ball straight at his

*Larwood: maintained he did not, as the Australian press claimed,
aim to maim batsmen with leg-theory.*

body. He commented that this type of reporting was typical of what appeared in the Australian papers and he doubted whether Richardson himself had actually said such a thing.

"It was rubbish," Harold said, "because you only have to think for a moment – if you're running in to bowl fast and you have a clear view of a set of stumps and the batsman is nowhere near them you'd be mad not to aim at clean-bowling him. And if he was taking guard a foot outside his leg stump then he would have to be actually standing about two feet outside. What possible reason could I have for bowling at him if he was standing so wide of the stumps? Certainly with Bradman if I sensed he was planning to move to leg at the last moment then I would shift the angle at him to prevent that luxury but nothing more than that."

The Australian media are masters at contriving and distorting a situation and then whipping it up into a national furore. They are particularly adept at this if they feel they can target a prominent individual. In 1972 the Australian media had Frank Sinatra in their sights due entirely to some innocuous tongue-in cheek comments he made about the standards of some reporters. The local media immediately went into overdrive distorting the comments as having been specifically aimed at Australian journalists. Sinatra said he had been speaking in general terms and wasn't talking about Australia at all. However nothing could quell the media blood-lust who then mobilised the whole trade union movement to black-ban the remainder of his tour. The whole schimozzle eventually fizzled out but it was a graphic example of the manner in which the Australian media can behave. Australia was then more mature by some forty years but it seems to have been the same tactic that was used on Jardine, an innocuous comment was distorted and reported as an anti-Australian slight which is very much what Jack Hobbs had described in 1933. The Sinatra furore did not pass unnoticed overseas. Helen Reddy, an Australian singer who had achieved some global fame, voiced her embarrassment when she appeared on Johnnie Carson's *The Tonight Show* in Los Angeles. Reddy had never met Sinatra but she said she was ashamed of the "gutter standards in journalism that are giving Australia a bad reputation." The next day she received a dozen yellow roses with a note saying: 'If anyone ever hits you, call me.'

Anything different or unable to be understood is likely to be a target for the Australian Press. In the early 1990s the Malaysian High Commissioner to Australia had an official title that included his own plus his father's Malaysian honorifics. This produced a full title of some six or seven words, a perfectly normal custom in that country. However, when a letter from the High Commissioner explaining some point appeared in the *Sydney Morning Herald*, the paper soon published a reader's letter that sneered and poured scorn on anyone with a name of such length, saying that nobody with that sort of name could be taken seriously. There will always be ignorant, insular people in any country, and the writer of the letter concerned probably thought he was being funny. But the remarkable aspect of this particular issue was that the *Sydney Morning Herald* felt the letter to be worthy of publishing. It says something about the philosophy of that newspaper that it did so without apparent thought for the gratuitous insult to a neighbouring Asian country and a gentle Malay culture going back a thousand years. A recent example of the lengths to which the media will go involved the 2005 jailing in Indonesia of an Australian woman convicted of drug running. This provoked the most furious and intemperate reaction in the media with one radio station likening the brown-skinned Indonesian President and judges to banana-eating apes. This comment evoked barely a ripple in Australia but it was an example of what Singapore's Lee Kuan Yew calls this short-sighted and parochial policy of "publish and be damned."

The Bradman mantra continues even today. In 2003 an article appeared in the *Sydney Morning Herald* saying that Bradman gave England an everlasting inferiority complex. The rationale for this theory was that public schools such as Eton, Harrow, Winchester and Marlborough were totally obsessed with batting because it was only through batting that a gentleman could reveal his true character and thus the innate superiority of English culture throughout the world. According to this theory boys at British public schools were taught how to bat, but not how to bowl, because the latter was not considered necessary for a gentleman. The article went on to say that the English felt that no batsman could consistently score runs with just untutored physical talent. Such an idea ignored the untutored, English, natural physical talent of cricketers such as Hobbs, Woolley, Hendren, Mead, Hammond or Sutcliffe with not a public school education amongst them, who somehow managed to total some 333,000 runs at an average of 50. That batting should require more coaching attention than bowling is perfectly logical and is merely because the majority of batting strokes are not natural for most people as they have to be taught and learned through practice. The natural stroke for any boy when first handed a bat is to grip it like an axe and play a baseball slog in the direction of mid-wicket.

Bowling is quite different and can be picked up by an individual with reasonable talent far more easily without the guidance of a coach, even though it requires practice to achieve real skill. The difference between learning the two is really just as simple as that. The article alleged the English had felt incredibly humiliated by Bradman because he was a batsman and not merely a bowler. It was a level of thought that seemed to demonstrate the apparent need to consistently measure everything in the world in terms of beating England. It also again revealed the Australian attitude that defeat in itself is humiliating and it showed the difficulty in understanding let alone accepting that England did not feel humiliated by Bradman. The truth was that the English cricket crowds who watched his mammoth run-making were not resentful but were amazed and applauded his feats as would any cricket crowd in Australia.

Sledging is actually praised in the Australian Press as being an Australian tradition. Grudging concession that sledging does occur might have been expected, but a 2005 editorial in the *Sydney Morning Herald* stated:

> In the gentlemen's game a capacity for endless obscenity gives you the edge. Australia's domination of world cricket has been built, in part, on a fearsome capacity for saying rude things to opponents' faces. People who don't like sledging should turn a deaf ear.

The Editorial continued to state that those who complain have no respect for tradition and it finished with the words:

> If you don't like it, then don't listen.

Rather than taking pride in what was right, the driving rationale appears to have been merely an instinct for what had been successful. It seemed to say: 'We'll use any tactic we can if it helps us win.' Australian success with this tactic was further celebrated in a recent *Sydney Morning Herald* article by Australian author Thomas Keneally who jeered at what he described as England's 'gentlemanly outrage over sledging.' In point of fact there is not a cricketing country in the world that has agreed with the

Australian tactic but most have felt they have to fight fire with fire and have responded in like fashion. It would appear that anything even vaguely perceived as gentlemanly is regarded as effected and lacking in masculinity and is the target of sneering comment, so perhaps Keneally's jibe should come as no surprise. In modern parlance the word gentlemanly is generally accepted as meaning civilized, courteous, obliging, well-mannered, etc, but in some quarters it still appears to be regarded as snobbish and effete and is therefore, in itself, 'un-Australian.' This attitude may explain the style of Thomson's rejection of Cowdrey's proffered hand as described in Chapter Two.

To bring the colour of the Australian Press up to date, we need look no further than the September 2006 death of Australian Steve Irwin. Irwin had achieved a degree of global exposure through a circus-like act whereby he wrestled with crocodiles and snakes and generally exposed himself to peril for the benefit of the cameras. He finally went too far in one of his escapades and when swimming within a couple of feet of a stingray was killed by its barb. Almost the whole of Australia went into national mourning, and the Queensland Government offered a State Funeral (which his widow was wise enough to decline). However, when England-based feminist and social commentator Germaine Greer put matters into more balanced perspective in an article in the *Guardian* she was subjected to the most vicious attack in Australia's only national daily *The Australian* in which she was described as 'a bitchslapping, poorly-sketched caricature of a harridan, an unwashed and wretched bag-lady and a childless feral hag'. What had provoked such intemperate fury by *The Australian*? The paper had likened Irwin's death to the passing of John F Kennedy or Princess Diana, which may be why Greer was suggesting there had been a degree of over-reaction. Quite simply Irwin had achieved some world attention and Australia and the media in particular had basked in the reflected superficial glamour of his performances and reputation. Greer had not actually criti-cised Irwin, but she had portrayed the Australian response from a detached practical standpoint and had committed the cardinal sin of criticising the country's reaction. Like Bradman, Irwin had been elevated to iconic, saint-like status, and because of this she had brought down on herself a torrent of offensive language.

*Australian openers Bill Woodfull and Bill Ponsford stride out
to the middle to face Leg-theory.*

As Jack Fingleton wrote in 1946:

It can be of no lasting good to any game if an individual is thought
to be the greater. Did it mean that Bradman, by his huge scores, by
his consistency in producing century after century, had dulled the
cricket appetite of the Australian crowds for anybody else than
Bradman?

It was for nothing more than such a trivial transgression that Greer was targeted in this manner in 2006, but the treatment she received from the Australian press does put into an understandable perspective the national reaction some seventy years earlier when Bradman was brought down to earth.

Perhaps we should have a look at Leg-Theory and/or Bodyline from a technical standpoint to see just what the fracas was all about.

LEG-THEORY – WAS IT
SO IMPOSSIBLE?

"I have a feeling that if Larwood and leg-theory had been
Australian the crowds there would have laughed and
applauded had our men been discomforted."

Jack Hobbs, 1933

"Verity maintained that Larwood rationed his bouncers –
'not 1 in 25 overs' – and felt that the Australians had
no real cause for complaint."

Verity's Biographer Alan Hill, 1986

LEG-THEORY INVOLVED FAST bowling, at times slightly short of a
length, the ball arriving thigh or waist high and aimed at the leg stump so
as to prevent the batsman from playing safely almost any stroke other than
on the leg side. It was the sort of tactic that would only work with a sufficiently fast and accurate bowling attack, otherwise, it would be expensive.
As Harold Larwood explained, "You only had to drift a little too far to leg
and be a bit off length and you were meat for a good bat".

It was hostile and, if not actually intimidating, it was certainly
inhibiting but then bowling of exceptional pace always has been. The
Australian Spofforth – bowling on very unpredictable wickets – was not
called 'The Demon' for nothing. One only has to consider the array of
bruises and broken limbs caused by the Australian pair of Gregory and
McDonald in the early 1920s to prove that point and as Maurice Leyland once

famously observed, "None of us likes fast bowling but some of us don't let on." Leg-theory was designed to limit the options open to the batsman and induce the false stroke and the speed and accuracy with which the ball was delivered was crucial in making it work. The batsman had only a split second in which to decide whether to move to leg and play to the off-side (with the risk of a catch in the slips), attempt a defensive shot or play to the leg-side, both of the latter choices being fraught with the danger of a ring of lurking short-leg fieldsmen. Finally, the tactic of bowling at where the batsman was standing was to force some sort of stroke to be played and not allow the batsman the luxury of choosing whether or not to play a shot.

It has been said that leg-theory or bodyline, according to the Australian press, exploded unexpectedly onto the cricket world in 1932 and that Douglas Jardine was the sole, evil architect and director of this form of assault. That is not true and in any event it is a simplistic and tendentious view of things. Writing in 1935, Herbert Sutcliffe stated that nothing would ever have been heard of fast leg-theory, nor would there have been a need for it if perfect wickets had not been produced that made good length fast bowling innocuous. Sutcliffe went on to say that he had faced Larwood's fast leg-theory attack on a number of occasions and did not mind it one little bit. This opinion seems to have been overlooked. Leslie Ames in his autobiography *Close of Play* published in 1953, said he had felt genuinely sorry for fast bowlers like Larwood, Voce, Allen and Bowes, called upon to bowl their hearts out on the unresponsive featherbed wickets of County cricket. To that opinion can be added the views of Bill Bowes whose opinion as one of the fast bowlers concerned in 1932/33 merits consideration. In his 1949 book *Express Deliveries* he explained:

> Any ball pitched outside the off stump could be left alone. If it whipped in and hit them on the pads the batsman did not need to worry about being given out LBW, for in those days one of the rules for an LBW decision was that the ball must pitch in line from wicket to wicket. With bats held high above their heads and without any semblance of a stroke they could let the off-theory bowlers waste their energy on the thin air. The only time they had any need to play the bowling was when it was coming directly at the body. So

the leg glance or the push to wide of mid-on became their chief scoring shots.

Leg-theory then was a natural development in cricket; but as bowled by Larwood with his extra pace and splendid direction it put him in a class on his own. When Allen, Voce or I dug a ball into the pitch it bounced rather like a tennis ball with much of the pace taken out of it. Larwood, hurling 'em down at express speed secured the ricochet which did not deprive the ball of its speed, at least not to the same extent.

Adding to this was an element within cricket that actually applauded the use of his pads by a batsman to protect his wicket. Writing in 1920, Donald Knight, Oxford and Surrey, wrote a chapter on batsmanship for the Badminton Library in which he openly stated:

There is nothing wrong or contrary to the spirit of the game in bringing the legs back together in front of the wicket and behind the bat to act as an extra defence so long as the ball has pitched off the wicket. When leaving the ball alone it is strongly advisable to keep the bat well up in the air above the head and cover the unguarded wicket with both legs.

Leg-theory had been successfully developed in the 1920s by the Worcestershire bowler Fred Root. In his book *The Bodyline Controversy*, Le Quesne doubts Root's influence on the basis that he was 'little if at all above medium pace'. This is an interesting opinion because the Cricinfo website describes Root's bowling as 'fast-medium', as does the *Who's Who of Cricketers*. Both also use the same term to describe the bowling of Bedser, Bailey and Botham. It would seem therefore that Root was distinctly quick-ish rather than merely humdrum medium-paced. If Root was little above medium pace it was remarkable that he caused such consternation amongst the Australians at Edgbaston in June 1926. Bowling for the North of England he took 7 for 42 with his leg-theory, his victims being Bardsley, Woodfull, Ponsford, Gregory, Ryder, Andrews and Taylor – Australia were 'Rooted' for 105. It is difficult to imagine the Australians losing seven wickets to gentle medium pace.

So worried were the Australians by his style of attack that having been selected for what amounted to a Test Trial at Lords, England v. The Rest, at the last moment he was made twelfth man for what Warner explained to him were 'diplomatic reasons'.

Warner told him that Warwick Armstrong and Clem Hill had arrived at the ground and had asked for seats behind the bowler's arm. "Their object," said Warner, "is to see how English batsmen play your leg-theory. My object is to stop them."

Although by then Root was 36 years old this performance earned him Test selection that summer; in two Tests he took 8 wickets at an average of 24. It is possible his age told against him for even though he played until 1932 he was not picked again for England. It seems to have been overlooked that the Australians were apparently so impressed with this style of attack, particularly following their experience at Edgbaston, that Root said he was offered a position in Australia to teach them how to bowl it. Writing in the *Sydney Sun* in January 1933, he said:

I was offered a job in Australia to teach leg-theory after my suc-cesses at Edgbaston. The Australians themselves have done every-thing to learn it. Australian scouts watched every game I played in 1926, but never learned to play it. It is ridiculous for the Australians to talk of retaliation when their bowlers have never previously practised it.

Considering all the protests against leg-theory one would think this statement from Root would have been quickly and firmly denied but it wasn't. Was it quietly ignored because it might have provoked Root to produce evidence supporting his claim? It seems strange that a published statement such as this, and at that time, was left to quietly wither without comment.

Given the way cricket was developing at that time, leg-theory or something like it, was inevitable, as Illingworth & Gregory say in their book *The Ashes*. Some new form of bowling attack would have been thought out and if the LBW law and pitches were not enough of a problem for bowlers, along came Bradman who had evolved an almost chanceless and risk-less style of batting. Bradman was not a batsman in the conventional mould who relaxed a little after passing his century. He was a relentless, clinical and self-absorbed accumulator of runs, more Swiss or Swedish in his cool detached approach, and a personality who had Australians marvelling and celebrating the runs he scored for them but not too sure about the detached teetotal man himself. But accumulate runs he did and once past his century he would just take fresh guard for the next century and the next and once even another. As Harold Larwood said, "He batted as if he had a point to prove."

The massive impact of his runs can be gauged by the fact that in the 36 Ashes Test matches in which he played from 1928 to 1948, 17 were won by Australia, nine were drawn and England won ten. However, of the 17 Australian victories there were only four where Bradman did not make a significant score and of the ten losses, only two where he did make a sizeable contribution. In 56 completed innings against England he accumulated 5,028 runs at an average of 89.78. It is probably true to say, though, that whilst the number of runs would be recalled, Bradman was never the sort of stylist who would have inspired writers such as Neville Cardus and he was not a batsmen of the eloquence of Trumper, Woolley, Hammond or McCabe. However, be that as it may, supreme stylist or not, Bradman was a run-making machine and the pitches and LBW law made it easier for him. Runs were runs no matter how they were accumulated. In Bradman, opposing teams and not just England, found themselves presented with a problem; however for most problems there is a solution – somewhere.

Plum Warner was so concerned that following Bradman's 334 in the third Test at Leeds in 1930, he wrote: 'England must evolve a new type of bowler and develop fresh ideas, strategy and tactics to curb his almost uncanny skill.' After Bradman's 232 in the fifth Test, Warner was to comment further: 'One trembles to think what lies in store for bowlers during the next 15 to 20 years.'

It has been stated by others that Jardine's leg-theory tactic was developed solely for the purpose of stymying Bradman. Jardine himself in his book *In Quest of the Ashes* refuted this, but agreed that if the opposition's chief run-scorer is inhibited then it is reasonable to assume that the other batsmen will be too. Asked if Bradman were the sole target, Harold Larwood said that was not true. "We bowled leg-theory in the first Test and Bradman wasn't even playing," he said. "Not only that, if it was only Bradman it was designed for then we would not have bowled leg-theory when he wasn't at the wicket would we?" Larwood went on to explain that he felt leg-theory had been developed not solely because of Bradman's run-scoring but also because of the LBW law in force then and the fact that in Australia the ball swung for a much shorter time due to the fact that Australian pitches took the shine off the ball sooner. He reckoned leg-theory would have been tried, with or without Bradman. He went on to say that the problem had been discussed between fast bowlers for some time in England because they felt that the LBW law disadvantaged them the most. "When the ball has stopped swinging," he said, "what other tactic did a fast bowler have? There was no point in bowling a break-back or off-cutter because the batsman could just pad up and you'd be wasting your time."

Larwood's explanation appears to be confirmed by his own bowling figures. Of his 162 wickets in the 1932 County season, only three were LBW, i.e. less than 2 per cent. To demonstrate that this figure was not unusual, the seven County seasons from 1926 to 1932 show that he took 882 wickets of which only 25, just under 3 per cent, were LBW decisions. The figures for all other bowlers were roughly similar. As if to prove the point, after the LBW law was changed Larwood's figures for the County seasons 1935 to 1937 show that of his 291 wickets, 29 were LBW, i.e. 10 per cent. Bowlers could now obtain wickets from balls pitched outside the off-stump, cutting back to strike the batsmen in front of their wicket and in line between the two sets of stumps with the ball, in the opinion of the umpire, going on to hit his stumps. Larwood's point of view was supported in the *Sydney Sun* just after the Adelaide Test in 1933. In an article headed 'Batsmen to Blame', the paper stated:

It is indeed strange that the inevitable introduction of fast leg-theory was not generally foreseen. The blame, if any, must rest on the batsman. He has asked for it with increasing insistence, from season to season, by refusing to be bowled when the ball has beaten the bat. It now has to beat the pads before it hits the stumps. Batting stance has changed. Instead of the firm right foot which 30 years ago the schoolboys coach would love to have had clamped, the first move in a protective shot is a step into the wickets with the right foot, so as to have the pad behind the bat in case the implement is beaten.

Another angle was put forward by Jack Fingleton in his book *Cricket Crisis* when he wrote:

Bradman could not have foreseen when he first committed himself to big scores, unlimited, that they would create bodyline and that he would reap the retribution of his own mastery. The people to blame for bodyline in the main were those who could see no further than huge scores, doped wickets and limitless Tests.

According to West Indian author Undine Giuseppi, Bill Voce bowled what she describes as 'bodyline' on the MCC tour of the West Indies in 1929/30 with West Indian batsman Clifford Inniss being knocked out cold in the process. The West Indies made no complaint at that time although when Learie Constantine later tried the same tactic the England captain, (The Hon) Freddie Calthorpe, publicly complained that such bowling was "not cricket". In one of the frequent quirks of the English selectors, Larwood was overlooked for that tour, so the prospect of the opening Test tandem of Larwood and Voce was yet to come. However whether Larwood would have bowled the same leg-theory on that tour as Voce we shall never know.

R H Lyttelton published his book *The Crisis in Cricket* in 1928 and pointed out the change that had taken place in the batsmen's stance at the wicket declaring that neither Spofforth nor Turner could have obtained the wickets they did against the current style of batting and LBW rule.

The pads, twice as protective as 20 years ago, comprise the second line of defence.

Australian author Jack Pollard in the *The Bradman Years* stated that leg-theory was deliberately malicious, delivered with the evil intent to cause harm. As has been noted, it was hostile, yes; intimidating, perhaps;

Harold Larwood (left) and Bill Voce: Nottinghamshire fast bowlers who were the major exponents of leg-theory on the tour. However, Voce had bowled in a similar style on the 1929/30 tour of the Caribbean, so was this in fact nothing new?

yet both of these descriptions are apt only because of the extreme pace of Larwood. Anyone who knew Larwood would also know that, professional or not, he would not have been a party to anything he felt was deliberately intended to be malevolent. When this comment was discussed with him, Harold was quite indignant at the accusation saying that he was aware this allegation had been made but that nothing could be further from the truth. "When you bowl fast," he said, "occasionally a batsman will be struck by a ball - it's unavoidable - but I never in my life ever bowled with the intention of inflicting injury." He added that if he had thought that injury to the batsman was Jardine's planned tactic, he would have protested to him about it, even though it would have annoyed Jardine. "The aim of leg-theory was only to take wickets. What would be the point of trying to achieve anything else?"

One fact emerged about his bowling during our chats which illuminated the kind of control that Larwood had over a cricket ball. It was the kind of control which gave his skipper confidence that he could maintain enough consistency to make the tactic stick over an entire series. After all what use was leg-theory if the bowlers could not bowl it well enough? Harold told me that when bowling an out-swinger, he held the seam upright, but the ball fairly loosely in his hand. For the in-swinger the only change was to hold the ball tightly, with the ball still remaining vertical. That was all there was to it, he said. It seems remarkable that a bowler of such feared speed and accuracy could have found such a simple method of making the ball move in different directions. The key, of course, would be the direction he set the ball off in when he released it at the top of his action and the accuracy of where he pitched the ball on the wicket, but the subtle difference in grip allowed him to disguise his intended delivery right to the last moment, giving the batsman as little time as possible to react. Add to that the surface with which the ball then came into contact and you have a potent weapon with which to attack any Test team's batting line-up.

The Australian press would have it that almost every ball Larwood, and indeed Bowes, delivered was pitched short and aimed to rear up at the heart of one of their batsmen. Far from it. In his biography of Hedley Verity *Portrait of a Cricketer* Alan Hill says that Verity's view was that Larwood rationed his bouncers, 'not 10 in 25 overs'. Verity has generally been held to be one of the most honest and thoughtful of cricketers and it seems odd that this description from him has not been quoted before.

Asked about the allegation of consistent bouncers, Larwood said this was a total fiction. "Practically all the bouncers," he said, "were caused entirely by pitches of dreadfully uneven and unpredictable bounce, not by deliberately bowling short. I aimed to get the ball to arrive at the batsman at about thigh or waist height and the fact that a number were even higher or much lower had nothing to do with what I was trying to achieve. It was just the pitch and you can't do much about that." This problem with the pitches is precisely what Bill Bowes described in his book *Express Deliveries*. He wrote:

> Deliveries pitching on the identical spot would come through differently, sometimes whizzing chest high or more, sometimes scarcely rising to half the height of the stumps. When batsmen like Woodfull and company went padding over and moved their right foot across the wicket as the natural counter to off-theory, they found that leg-theory Larwood had knocked their leg stump out of the ground behind their legs.

According to EW Swanton this description of the pitches was confirmed to him by Gubby Allen, who said: "Harold would drop three on the same spot: one would come through head high, the next hip high and the next chest high." All of this would seem to suggest that rather than leg-theory it was mostly the condition of the Australian pitches that was responsible for injuries sustained - a sort of friendly fire.

Indeed there is a double standard at work generally speaking. For example Jack Pollard, who alleged that Larwood was deliberately malicious, does not appear to have had his feelings roused in any way regarding fast, short-pitched bowling when Lillee and Thomsom were at work in the 1970s. Indeed Lillee went into print with the words:

> I want it to hurt so much the batsman will not want to face me any more.

Add to those sentiments the comment made by Jeff Thomson that he couldn't wait to 'split a stiff upper lip' and you have the same situation as allegedly occured in 1932/33 - that one side wanted to hurt the other as a means to winning.

Where was the condemnation then?

In his book *Ashes in the Mouth* English author Ronald Mason appears to applaud the vicious attack of Lillee and Thomson describing the two as nothing more than 'gifted and vigorous individualists thirsting for blood, honour and glory.'

Was Harold Larwood not also a "gifted individualist"?

Larwood went on to make a comparison between himself and Bill Voce, who was a left-arm bowler. He said there was very little difference between the field that Voce would normally bowl to with the new ball with leg-slips, a short-leg, etc., compared with his field for leg-theory, because being left-handed, Voce usually swung the ball across or into the right hand bat anyway. Larwood said that he reckoned not many people had realised this or if they had it had been ignored. According to Undine Giuseppi, this view was supported by Learie Constantine who said that no bowler of body-line ever set out to maim a man, but rather to intimidate him first, to make him aware the ball can be made to do something and as a result of that intimidation to bowl him out. He cited the example of Larwood bumping deliberately at the West Indian batsmen in 1928 which he said resulted in the batsmen who flinched, getting out. Those who hit the ball stayed in. "And that," said Constantine, "is really all there was to it."

In Larwood, England had a quite exceptional bowler in terms of speed accuracy and stamina. In Bill Voce they had another fairly unique bowler. Voce was then only 23 years of age and he was tall, 6 foot 3 inches in height and was left-handed. He was not as fast as Larwood, but bowling accurately over or round the wicket he was the natural leg-theory foil for the other end to Larwood. Voce had burst upon the County scene aged 19 in 1929, taking 120 wickets over the season. His weapons were speed, swing and more than usual bounce due to his height. However, it should not be thought that Larwood and/or Voce themselves had no input into the style of attack England chose. Harold stated that on occasion he would suggest to Jardine that maybe it was time to switch to leg-theory. "It did not always come from Mr Jardine," he said. "We were professionals and he was the skipper, but you know we weren't just puppets on a string. We made our own sugges-tions." This is an interesting comment that contrasts with the widely promoted view that Jardine and only Jardine directed when leg-theory should be used.

Bill Woodfull is struck at Adelaide. Undoubtedly it was the uneven bounce which caused the Australian captain to duck into the delivery from Larwood, which was, in any case, outside off stump when it struck him squarely in the chest, near his heart.

The unpredictable bounce was undoubtedly what was responsible for the ball that struck Woodfull near his heart in the third Test. He thought it was going to be a bouncer, but it didn't rise as expected and Woodfull ducked into it. Larwood was bowling outside the off stump at the time and the culprit was entirely the pitch, not Larwood, nor leg-theory. The local media reported it as the malicious aggression of bodyline, but that was not the case. The preparation and production of the pitches on which Test matches are to be played is always the responsibility of the host country and neither Jardine nor Larwood could be held accountable for the behaviour of the pitches on which they had to play. The remedy lay in the hands of the Australian cricket authorities themselves, but their ground curators seem to have been negligent or casual in their approach and failed to solve the problem. It is possible that because none of the Australian bowlers were of any real pace, unpredictable bounce may not have been regarded as a serious problem, but if this was the reason for ignoring this factor, it rebounded on them when Larwood was delivering. Either way the Australian cricket authorities must have realised the manner in which their own pitches were making the bowling of Larwood even more difficult to play. The problem of uneven bounce or under-prepared pitches was one that even came to the attention of MCC, whose President, Viscount Lewisham, suggested the Australians be cabled:

> If Australian Board consider that Larwood too fast a bowler to be safe on present Australian wickets Marylebone feel sure that Jardine would give the utmost consideration to their view.

However well intended, it was an offer of almost naïve innocence, virtually saying, 'Just let us know if we're too fast and we'll slow it down for you.'

The one possible exception to this was the Melbourne pitch for the second Test. Melbourne had a reputation for being hard and fast, well-suited to fast bowlers and consequently Jardine selected four quicks for that match. The pitch turned out to be much slower than usual and more favourable to spin and it was only on this much slower pitch that Bradman was able to make something approaching his expected runs. Perhaps the groundsman there had realised what the rest of his counterparts did not and prepared a surface more suitable to his own side. We will never know for sure.

There were naturally enough rumours that the pitch had been 'doctored' to slow it down and although this cannot be proven the thoughts are understandable when a pitch, just for one match, changes its usual character. From an Australian standpoint, Jack Fingleton has also conceded:

> Had Bradman been an Englishman and whipped the Australians as he did the English, the Australians would have been tempted to use some such drastic theory against Bradman.

The Australian website *334notout* takes issue with the concept that the tactic was logical, saying that under Woodfull there was never any suggestion of retaliation. This misses three crucial points:

- It was not a question of retaliation, but merely of using a specific and unique bowling talent – which Australia just did not possess.
- 'It was only common sense' – see Bob Wyatt comment later.
- Woodfull could hardly have said anything else.

The same website goes on to say:

Although the majority of wickets to fall were non-bodyline, the fact that the pressure had been put on the batsmen by these tactics could not have helped their state of mind.

Quite possibly so, but that is frequently the effect of great speed. What of the pressure put on the English batsmen by the lightning lifting deliveries of Lillee and Thomson during the 1974/75 series? The word 'retaliate' carrying with it the connotation of repayment of injury or insult appears to have been used by that website to support the moral high ground sought in the original complaint to MCC by the Australian Cricket Board. They simply did not possess the wherewithal to implement the same style of attack as the English and therefore could not do so. In his book *The Bodyline Controversy* Le Quesne featured a photograph of Woodfull being struck by the previously mentioned lifting ball and also in the picture is Bill Bowes standing with his hands on his hips at what the caption says is forward short-leg, see opposite. Le Quesne comments that the picture did much to form the Australian image of bodyline and goes on to say that Bowes' stance 'exhibits a typical Yorkshire degree of sympathy. This statement implies that Bowes cared nothing for injuries sustained by the Australian batsmen. As the photograph appears to have been taken at the split second when Woodfull was actually struck, Bowes would not have had time to make any move. However, what would another photograph, taken a second or so later, have revealed? Possibly a fielder moving towards the batsman with some concern? Harold Larwood said he recalled seeing the photograph before, but, when asked about the Le Quesne implication, his response was:

Just not true! Of course we were concerned when anybody got hurt. In any event you know Bill Bowes wasn't the fastest chap in

The picture which did much to form the Australian image of 'Bodyline'. However, note the position of Woodfull's feet, outside the off stump, and even then he appears to be moving backwards. As for the leg trap, Jardine did not play in this match against an Australian XI at Melbourne and Harold Larwood's opinion was that Bill Bowes (pictured at short leg) was not sharp enough to field close in if he was bowling leg-theory. In fact Bowes took just one catch during the whole tour. Once again the real culprit seems to have been the unpredictable wicket.

the field and if you look at that picture there's no other short-legs and I reckon Bill was at shortish mid-wicket not short leg. He never fielded in my leg trap, he wasn't sharp enough and that ball was simply another case of the pitch being unpredictable. That ball wasn't short, it just reared up. In fact we weren't bowling leg-theory at the time.

Considering the cluster of short-legs usually positioned for leg-theory this opinion appears valid. To add to this impression Woodfull, if anything, appears to be outside his off-stump, so the ball could hardly have been bowled on the line of leg. Moreover of England's total of 131 catches taken on that tour, Bowes managed only one, so it is unlikely he would have been placed in a specialist position such as short-leg. The photograph did, however, neatly fit the propaganda which Le Quesne wished to disseminate, which propagated the various popular theories and demonised several members of the England team. It is undoubtedly painful to look at as one imagines the shock Woodfull must have felt at being hit by a ball moving at upwards of 90mph, but the connotation given to the picture seems to have been entirely concocted for nefarious purposes.

Le Quesne also includes a photograph featuring a leg-theory delivery (see p87) for which his caption was:

Jardine - at square leg, in characteristic posture - calculates the effect of it.

This is a preposterous statement. Does a good captain not calculate the effectiveness of every ball bowled? In fact in the photograph every fielder in the leg-trap is intent on watching the ball and that is surely logical. A catch, after all may have been coming their way.

That leg-theory could be played was demonstrated by Stan McCabe's wonderful innings of 187 not out in the first Test. Previous books on the subject have tended to dismiss this innings as a one-off fluke, possibly because McCabe's subsequent innings during the series never measured up to it. Bradman and Fingleton were dismissive, although that looks as though it may have been from a need to portray leg-theory as un-playable. Certainly neither Fingleton, nor Bradman in particular, would have wanted to concede that one batsman could achieve what they couldn't. Moreover, if leg-theory could be played wouldn't that totally undermine the complaints about the tactic? Some authors have written that the success of McCabe's performance was largely due to the fact that Larwood did not bowl leg-theory to him. Asked about this version of events, Larwood's retort was that it was "bloody nonsense. Of course we bowled leg-theory to Stan," he said. "Why would we have singled him out for special treatment?"

Arthur Mailey was a spectator at the first Test at Sydney, and he supported this when he wrote that one of the main factors for Australia's defeat in that Test was 'the inability of the Australians to play fast leg-theory bowling'. He would hardly have made that comment had leg-theory not featured in the match he had just watched. In his book *Farewell to Cricket* Bradman produced figures to demonstrate that during the series and through unorthodox methods he was able to achieve a reasonable batting average. He quotes the four Tests in which he played (he didn't appear in the first Test) and compares his figures with those of McCabe and Richardson who he said were the only other Australian batsmen able to counter leg-theory. The figures he quotes are as follows:

	Innings	Runs	Not Out	Highest Score	Average
Bradman	8	396	1	103*	56.57
Richardson	8	230	0	83	28.70
McCabe	8	166	0	73	20.70

At first sight the figures seem to support Bradman's claim that he was head and shoulders above anyone else. However he had excluded McCabe's runs in the first Test where he made his famous 187 not out, plus 32 in the second innings.

Therefore, with McCabe's runs included, the full position for the entire series was actually as follows:

	Innings	Runs	Not Out	Highest Score	Average
Bradman	8	396	1	103*	56.57
Richardson	10	279	0	83	27.90
McCabe	10	385	1	187*	42.77

* Not Out

McCabe played two more innings than Bradman and it may be argued that it was only one significant innings that Bradman had excluded from his figures, but one innings can make a considerable difference to an average for a Test series. For instance if Bradman's one innings of 103 not out is removed from the total runs he scored, his average then drops to 41.85. It should also be noted that Bradman's innings of 103 was made on a remarkably slow pitch at Melbourne where the England attack had their teeth drawn. Could this be the Don trying to re-write history?

In the determination to demonstrate that leg-theory was impossible to

Le Quesne used this photograph as evidence to damn Douglas Jardine as the demon of Bodyline. It shows Bill Woodfull ably ducking a bouncer from Harold Larwood during the fourth Test at Brisbane.

play another factor consistently overlooked has been the matter of Stan McCabe's rapidly deteriorating health. He was never constitutionally robust and his condition seriously worsened as the series progressed, culminating in the removal of his tonsils after the fifth Test. Whether the source of the problem was tonsillitis or quinsy (a throat-abscess secondary to acute tonsillitis) is not known, but whatever it was it proved a serious problem against which McCabe battled through the series, delaying the operation as long as possible. It should be remembered that because the 1930s pre-dated the advent of antibiotics, the symptoms of throat pain coupled with high fever and headaches would have made playing on a hot cricket field increasingly difficult to handle. Having to endure these debilitating health problems, which would not necessarily have been perceptible to others, would have significantly reduced McCabe's ability to perform as normal. His innings of 187 was made on 2/3 December 1932. Other than one innings of 73 in the last Test on 23 February 1933 his batting deteriorated during the intervening eleven weeks. For a throat problem serious enough to eventually require surgery, a lengthy postponement could only have exacerbated the condition. However even with that to contend with McCabe was dismissed by Larwood only once in his ten innings. By comparison the fully fit Bradman succumbed to Larwood four times out of seven dismissals. The fact that McCabe's tonsils seriously affected his batting is confirmed by Maurice Tate in his book *My Cricketing Reminiscences*. Tate wrote:

> My impression was that if McCabe had played all through the other Tests as he did in this innings, he would have hit "bodyline" all over the place. Unfortunately he had to have his tonsils out, and this affected his health sufficiently to make him lose his best form.

Harold Larwood confirmed this opinion. In fact so serious was McCabe's condition that he was operated on immediately after the last Test. Asked about this some sixty years later Larwood said Stan McCabe was just about the only Australian batsman, Bradman apart, who was quick enough on his feet to handle leg-theory without too much difficulty. He added that he felt McCabe became noticeably less quick in his reflexes and footwork as the series progressed and that the England team had heard he had some problem, although they didn't know what it was. His observation would fit a man who was sick and battling his way through. "Make no mistake," Harold said, "that innings was no fluke. You can't make as many as 187 runs with just luck – and don't think we didn't try to get him out."

When Australian batsman Bill Brown, on the fringes of the side, but as yet uncapped in 1932/33, was interviewed in August 2006, he said:

> Stan McCabe played a beautiful innings in Sydney, which I saw: 187 not out. Stan was ideally suited against Bodyline. He had a beautiful square cut and hook shot. Those two shots were the main weapons against Bodyline. If you didn't have those shots it was hopeless. Stan would stand up there and cut and hook. The shorter you bowled at him the harder he hooked you.

From 1934 Brown played 22 Tests, had a batting average of 47 and was a member of the 1948 Invincibles. He knew what he was talking about and

Stan McCabe: had he been available for the entire series perhaps history would have a different view of the series.

believed that leg-theory could be played - if you had the footwork and shots. So, with Brown's backing, we can say that McCabe was one batsman who:

- had always relished fast bowling,
- was quick enough on his feet to handle leg theory, and
- without the increasing illness, would probably have successfully dealt with it.

Stan McCabe would average 60 in the 1934 Ashes series, 54 in 1936/37 and 45 in 1938. His career Test batting average of 48.21 puts him in the highest class. Larwood went on to say that he felt quite sure Archie Jackson, had he been available, would have been another whose footwork was such that he would have dealt with the English style of attack. In his words:

Archie was so quick that he could come down the wicket to me, and not many could do that. But most of the rest of them were far too flat-footed and two-eyed to handle real pace.

Any British journalist on the tour who did not totally condemn leg-theory as a tactic has subsequently been criticised, even lampooned. Jim Swanton, for instance, claimed that had he been there he would have raised an outcry against leg-theory. However he had plenty of opportunity in his writings of 1933, 1934 and later to make public his views on leg-theory, but interestingly he does not seem to have done so until after Jardine's death. His attitude towards Jack Hobbs was somewhat patronising. According to Swanton, Hobbs was only a professional and therefore in some fear of Jardine who was the amateur captain of Surrey. In point of fact, Hobbs was by far England's senior cricketer, 18 years older than Jardine and had been appointed to the Selection Committee in 1930. Hobbs was by nature a very mild-mannered man but writing of leg-theory he said:

Bearing in mind Larwood's great pace, ask yourself if the batsman is not intimidated. I know there is nothing in the rules against leg-theory and bodyline bowling. But I ask you!

One would have thought this was clear and critical enough, yet even this was not sufficient. Swanton derided Bruce Harris, author of the book *Jardine Justified*, as a man who had 'absolutely no cricket experience' and went on to quote Australian Gilbert Mant who, some sixty years after the tour, decided to write *A Cuckoo in the Bodyline Nest*. Mant had opined: 'Harris was merely a tennis writer who knew nothing whatsoever about cricket' and dismissed him as having been nothing more than a brainwashed disciple of Jardine. Again Swanton and Mant both made their comments after Bruce Harris had departed this world.

If one reads Harris's book it is very difficult indeed to get the impression that he knew 'nothing whatsoever about cricket'. It is not at all the

Archie Jackson: Larwood held few fears for the nimble-footed batsman.

whitewash claimed by Mant and Swanton and reads as if written by someone who certainly understood cricket. Perhaps he had a fair amount of cricket knowledge without having previously written about cricket and had suffi-cient perspicacity to see the broader picture. It seems highly unlikely that a newspaper of the reputation of the *Evening Standard* would have incurred the expense to send all the way to Australia a reporter who they were aware knew absolutely nothing about cricket. Bruce Harris may well have been employed by the *Evening Standard* to write about tennis, but that does not mean that cricket was a game of which he was completely lacking in any knowledge. Harris went on to write six acclaimed books about later Ashes series: 1936/37, 1946/47, 1950/51, 1953, 1954/55 and 1956 and was the founding secretary of the Cricket Writers' Club in 1947.

In his biography of Archie Jackson *The Keats of Cricket* David Frith recounts Jackson's view that bodyline could be played by batsmen fleet enough of foot. Jackson was not fit enough to be selected for the Australian

Test team (he died of tuberculosis on 16 February 1933), but it seems almost certain that he would have played if he had not been so sick. He had previously played Larwood quite fearlessly and in his foreword to Frith's book Larwood recalled an encounter during the fifth Test at the Oval in 1930 when Jackson came down the wicket and said to him:

> Well, Harold, it's only a game but what a grand one we're having today! I hope you're enjoying our battle as much as those spectators seem to be. You know you've hit me almost as many times as I've hit you! I wish you'd drop one a little off line occasionally.

Jackson was extremely quick on his feet, but his comment indicates a very different approach to Larwood and during the 1932/33 tour he was to state: "It is my belief that Larwood would not intentionally hurt a fly." Naturally, it cannot be said with total certainty how Jackson would have played Larwood's leg-theory had he not been laid low with tuberculosis, just as we do not know what McCabe's performances might have been had he not battled through with an increasingly severe throat problem. However what is known is that both of these batsmen were renowned for three aspects of their play: extremely quick reflexes, nimble footwork, and a liking for fast bowling. Harold Larwood was in no doubt, saying: "The Archie Jackson I knew in 1930 wouldn't have had too much trouble with leg-theory, he would have been quick enough to handle it." Perhaps they would have adopted the batting tactics suggested by Wyatt, who writing of Bradman, said:

> To Larwood I would have stood at least six inches outside the leg stump. The dangerous ball was the one which left you uncertain whether it was going to bounce or not. If you stood well outside the leg stump and it dropped short you were in a very good position to square-cut it. To a straight ball pitched well up you had to be quick enough to get in line, but then you could play it any way you wished. On many occasions Don drew away to square-cut the ball when he would have been better off if he had stood outside and then moved over. It would have made it unnecessary for him to

move his head so much. At the same time he would not have had to play any ball coming directly at or near him.

Shortly before the end of the third Test, the *Adelaide Advertiser* published the contents of a letter written to the Melbourne press by ex-Australia captain Monty Noble in which he pointed out, for the benefit of the Australian batsmen, the fallacy of attempting to play leg-theory. His advice was to allow any ball pitched outside the leg stump to go through to the keeper:

How often do we see batsmen, when a field is set for off-theory, allow the ball to pass to the keeper. Isn't it just as easy to allow it to pass when on the leg side, the field being packed on that side?

Noble was experienced enough for his views to have credence. Would a fully fit McCabe or Jackson have successfully played leg-theory that way? McCabe was 22 at the time and when Jackson died he was 23.

Two contemporary comments on the leg-theory are interesting, one made by Bill O'Reilly and reported by Australian author Jack McHarg and one made by Vic Richardson, as recounted by cricket writer and commentator, Alan McGilvray. According to McHarg, O'Reilly had said that if Bradman had been available for the first Test, teamed with McCabe, they might well have "seen off" bodyline for good. Given McCabe's innings in that game this is an intriguing statement, not for the idea that the two might have been able to handle leg-theory, that much is clear enough, but from the seeming implication that it was not the actual principle of leg-theory itself that was the problem, but rather whether or not it could be mastered.

McGilvray in similar fashion quotes Vic Richardson as saying that had he been able to stay with Stan McCabe a little longer as McCabe made his 187 not out in the first Test, he reckoned he might have killed off leg-theory before it really started. Once more it is not the strategy that appears to be questioned, but rather whether it could be handled. McGilvray also quotes Richardson as having frequently pleaded with Woodfull to attempt the same tactic with his own bowlers, but as McGilvray himself stated:

It is doubtful whether an Australian counter-offensive would have succeeded anyway. The tactics required great accuracy, and there was no Harold Larwood in the Australian team of the time.

As has been observed elsewhere, Woodfull was undoubtedly only too aware that an attempt at the same strategy would have been futile, expensive and something of an embarrassment. Just how do you fire the cannon-balls when you have no cannon?

O'Reilly's comment also appears to suggest that leg-theory was persisted with only because it was successful. To be blunt, the Australian batsmen could not cope with it. Had they been able to handle the tactic it stands to reason it would have been abandoned.

The interesting aspect of all this is the reaction this all provoked – namely: if we can handle it, there's no problem, but if we can't then we'll complain that it's unfair. Bill Brown said:

It was almost impossible to make runs consistently against them. You could get runs in small bursts, but in the main, no. The bowling was absolutely on top. Six men on the leg-side around the bat and the ball rising on the body all the time.

When placed in the context of his earlier description of Stan McCabe, Brown's comment seems to suggest once again that it was their inability to master leg-theory that was the root cause of the Australian complaint rather than any principle involved as has subsequently been painted.

Several authors have speculated that leg-theory was unnecessary because England would have won that series anyway. Those authors may not have noticed the opinion of Sheffield Shield cricketer and author Dick Whitington, who played in 54 matches for South Australia between 1932 and 1946 and had appeared in the match against MCC in November 1932, a match in which Larwood bowled only five overs due to injury. In his 1972 biography of Bill O'Reilly, Whitington recalled watching Larwood as follows:

I still remember Larwood, delivering to a normal field, bowling four balls of between 90 and 100 miles an hour just short of a length to The Don in the space of two overs. Don square-cut the first of them past point for four, hooked the second low past square leg for four, square-cut the third for four and hooked the fourth low again for four. From where I was sitting, each of the balls seemed identical in length and direction.

It only went to show what Bradman might have done to this attack had Jardine not employed Bodyline. I'd not even dreamt of hooking the yards slower Larwood of the MCC-South Australia game.

This is a straightforward opinion from the point of view of an experienced Sheffield Shield cricketer and author written 40 years later and would seem to give the lie to the idea that Bradman's run scoring could have been dealt with successfully by conventional means. What Whitington's opinion implicitly suggests is that Jardine's strategy was quite logical and well planned.

However, let us speculate on what might have been the position had Bradman been, say, South African, and had run riot through the English bowling for that country instead of for Australia. What if a South African batsman, Herbie Taylor for instance, a batsman good enough for a Test average of 40, had produced a succession of huge scores during the Series in 1927/28, 1929 and 1930/31, and had thus swung the results for South Africa off his own bat? If Jardine or Wyatt were the English captain to South Africa, would they have used the same leg-theory tactic in South Africa supposing they had had a bowler such as Larwood at their disposal? Given that the South African batsman would have posed exactly the same problem as Bradman, there does not appear to be any reason to suppose the same tactic would not have been put into operation. Whether it would have succeeded on South African pitches is a different matter. They are not quite as hard and unforgiving for fast bowlers as those in Australia, but the point should be emphasised that taking into account the factors of LBW laws etc., there does not appear to be any evidence that leg-theory was a specifically anti-Australia policy. It had already been tried in the West Indies and it merely came along as a natural evolution at that time. Australia just happened to be the place where it went into full and successful swing.

The question then should be asked, would the reaction have been the same? The cultural inheritance and social attitudes in South Africa were different from those of Australia, and particularly so at that time. There was not the same national obsession with sport or gambling and so we must ask whether there would have been the same injured outcry about matters of principle if South Africans found they could not handle leg-theory. European South Africa owed its origins to the founding of what was to become Cape Colony by the Dutch East India Company in 1652, and this settlement had gradually expanded inland. It was, therefore, a country of much longer standing than Australia and different in origin. Despite the Boer Wars, South Africa at that time did not seem to have the anti-English element that existed in Australia. It did not feel as remote and cut off from England and Europe as did Australia. It had British Rhodesia and the British-administered Protectorate of Bechuanaland immediately to the north. To the east was Portuguese Mozambique and to the west, British-administered South West Africa. It is possible that the South African reaction would have been to consider utilising the same tactic, although they too would probably have recognised that a bowler such as Larwood was the unique ingredient that made leg-theory so successful. Whether or not the South Africans would have raised the ante in the same fashion as the Australians when they found they were losing is, of course, something that can only be a matter for conjecture. But history proves that there do seem to have been a greater number of controversies in England-Australia matches than in any series between England and other cricketing countries.

For a final comment on leg-theory, let us consider the views of the four Yorkshiremen who were in Jardine's team. Later in life, Bob Wyatt recalled that on the ship taking most of the team from New Zealand to Canada there had been quite naturally a number of serious discussions about the tour and its various events and the issues raised. The four Yorkshiremen concerned were Herbert Sutcliffe, Maurice Leyland, Hedley Verity and Bill Bowes. According to Wyatt all four were unanimous in their support of Jardine's leg-theory tactic, believing that any batsman with guts could cope with it. Yorkshire has always had a less sentimental view of cricket – ironically more in line with the Australian attitude.

AUSTRALIAN TEST SELECTION

"While the Australian selectors were lamenting the scarcity of fast and medium-paced bowlers, the Englishmen were embarrassed owing to a superabundance of them."

Arthur Mailey, 1933

"Dropping Clarrie Grimmett was stupidity."

Bill O'Reilly, 1972

A COUNTRY'S ATTITUDE towards a strength possessed only by the opposition is frequently coloured by its own resources and very rarely will this reaction be impartial. When the googly, Bosie or wrong 'un – call it what you will – first appeared in the early 1900s, no less a cricketer than Arthur Shrewsbury, possibly the finest batsman in the world during the previous ten years, complained that it was unfair. It had not been seen before, and only one side had the ability to produce it (and, at the time, only one bowler, Bosanquet). Shrewsbury's complaint implied that it was 'unsportsmanlike'. This type of delivery, an off-break produced by what appeared to be a leg-break action, is difficult to bowl and the deliberate intention is to deceive the batsman, otherwise, the bowler might more easily merely bowl an off-break which the batsman would easily read.

And so deviousness made its first appearance on the cricket scene. Although that delivery was not intimidating, the googly, on the other hand, could be the cause of considerable embarrassment if a reputable batsman was publicly seen to have played totally the wrong shot.

In March 1903 the first googly in Australia was bowled by Bernard Bosanquet to Victor Trumper. At that point Trumper had made 40 runs in about 20 minutes and had worked up a head of steam. Bosanquet then bowled two leg-breaks, which Trumper stroked gracefully into the covers. Lulled into a false sense of security, to the third ball, a googly, pitched as for the previous two deliveries, Trumper played the same exquisite cover drive and had his middle stump removed.

Trumper does not appear to have complained, but there were others who did – and did so even more when other googly bowlers appeared on the scene, such as the South African quartet of Faulkner, Vogler, Schwartz and White in 1912. Some felt that it was surreptitious, somehow underhanded and therefore not cricket. It should be noted that none of the complaints emanated from sides that had one of these mystery bowlers in their own ranks.

The contention has always been that had Australia had the bowlers of suitable pace and ability, they would have undoubtedly employed the same successful tactic which was the cause of their downfall during the series. It is therefore worthwhile investigating just what sort of bowling attack Australia had at its disposal at that time. Arthur Mailey commented that England had plenty of good fast bowlers, while Australia had practically none. At the end of the series, he went on to write:

O'Reilly was a new bowler who was always a force to be reckoned with, but while Australia seems to be well supplied by promising batsmen, there seems to be a scarcity of bowlers fit to take their place in Test cricket.

It was perhaps just one of those strange coincidences that make cricket history fascinating, for Australia has usually been able to produce fast men without any problem. They may not have come off the consistent fast bowling assembly line that the West Indies seemed to have at one time, but in names such as Spofforth, Gregory, McDonald, Lindwall, Miller, McKenzie, Lillee, Thomson, McDermott, McGrath and, most recently, Lee, there is an array of some of the most successful fast bowlers in the history of Test cricket. These men did not appear one after another, yet even in between times, Australia has usually had bowlers of genuine talent, if not of top pace, to successfully fly the flag – men such as Davidson, Hawke, Connolly, Gilmour and Walker. The early 1930s, though, appears to have been a time of fast-bowling drought for Australia and, as Arthur Mailey wrote then, the nation's resources in this respect were the complete opposite of England's.

The Australian bowlers selected for the 1930 Ashes Series in England, were Wall (fastish), Hurwood (medium), Hornibrook (left-hand spin) and Grimmett, with support from all-rounders such as McCabe and Fairfax. In the event, Hurwood was not picked for any of the Tests, and Wall ended the series with only 13 wickets at 43.61. Without Grimmett, who took 29 wickets at 31.89, they would have been in something of a mess. The two all-rounders, McCabe and Fairfax, took 8 and 12 wickets respectively at about 27. As someone commented at the time, the 1930 Australians were, in effect, a two-man team – Bradman and Grimmett.

In 1928/29 and already aged nearly 46, the left-arm chinaman spinner, Ironmonger, made his Test debut, playing twice in the series. His performance was only moderate, taking 6 wickets at an average of 51. In 1930, the almost medium-paced leg-spinner O'Reilly emerged, but there was no-one to solve the problem of the opening bowling position. Ironmonger was a very successful bowler in Australia, as is attested by his Test record of 74 wickets at an average of 17.97, but was never selected for an official overseas tour because of a suspect action. O'Reilly was to develop into one of the greats, but for the slightly faster bowling of Ernie McCormick, the Australians had yet to wait a few years.

To open along with Wall in the first Test in 1932, the Australian selectors included Nagel, a very tall medium-pacer who had caused havoc amongst the English batting in a warm-up match between England and an Australian XI, when he had taken 8 for 32, bowling England out for 60 in their second innings. Nagel, who had produced significant swing and movement off the pitch on that occasion, achieved moderate success in the Test, but was immediately dropped and never again seen in the Test arena. The decision by the Australian selectors to drop him seems strange for, although Nagel took 2 for 110 in the Test, those two wickets were of the English century-makers Hammond and Pataudi, and his figures do not compare unfavourably with those of Wall, who took 3 for 104 or O'Reilly with 3 for 117. Moreover, Nagel was more economical than Wall and his height would have been an asset in the bounce he could produce.

Although none of the Australian bowlers achieved anything of note, Nagel appears to have been made the scapegoat, almost as if the Australian selectors felt some gesture was needed to mollify a disappointed public. Nagel was only 27 at the time, and thereafter he appears to have lost interest in first-class cricket, perhaps disillusioned by the treatment handed out to him by the Test selectors. Arthur Mailey commented at the time on this seemingly odd philosophy when he wrote:

There has been a tendency lately to pick a player who scores a century or obtains six wickets and drop him suddenly if he fails in his first match. Selectors who adopt these methods do not require judgment they only need a scoreboard.

One thinks of England in the late 1980s and 90s on reading that remark.

Mailey seems to have recognised at least one of the problems emerging in the Australian camp, that the selectors appeared to have chopped and changed with little in the way of a coherent plan. So how many of the problems faced by Australia during the 1932/33 series were caused by their own selection policies?

Although he was then nearly 51 years of age, Ironmonger was again re-introduced into the Australian Test squad for the second Test. He had formed a very successful team with Grimmett against the West Indies in 1930/31 and South Africa in 1931/32 and in the two series they had between them snared some 66 per cent of all wickets taken for Australia. But so bereft was Australia's fast bowling cupboard that Wall opened the bowling with leg-spinner O'Reilly in three of the remaining Tests. Admittedly, O'Reilly was a little quicker than the conventional leg-spinner, but it is rare for a leg-break bowler to open the bowling and this move does seem to highlight the fast-bowling problems faced by the Australian selectors.

It may well be that so successful had been the spin attack over the past several seasons that little attention was given to the lack of fast bowling talent. Not surprisingly, Australia did not again use the unusual tactic of

O'Reilly as an opening bowler until the first Test of the 1938 Series when Bradman decided O'Reilly should open the bowling with McCormick at Trent Bridge. England scored 658 for 8 wickets declared in that innings, and the experiment was discarded for good.

Tim Wall was to finish the Series with 16 wickets at 25.56. He came to England for the 1934 Series, but although playing in four of the Tests he ended with just 6 wickets at an average of 78.66. Wall's total Test figures against England of 43 wickets at an average of nearly 39 are indicative of a bowler who was not of the highest Test class. However Wall does also put the Australian batting resources against pace into an interesting perspective. The winner of the Sheffield Shield in 1932/33 was New South Wales. Wall who, as has been demonstrated, was only of average Test standard, nonetheless was good enough to take all 10 New South Wales first innings wickets for 36 runs for South Australia at Sydney in February 1933. Amongst his victims were Bradman and Fingleton, plus Brown and McCabe, the latter two each for a duck. In its obituary of Wall in 1981, *Wisden Cricket Monthly* described him as a nearly man, a great trier but not quite fast enough to really make it at Test level. However, the fact that he did take all 10 New South Wales wickets, admittedly into a brisk breeze which helped his swing, seems to suggest that Australian batsmen at that time did not have sufficient practice against pace of quality. This deficiency may have told against them when they encountered the fast and accurate English attack.

Other selection mysteries only made things worse. Such rashness appears to have set in that Grimmett was dropped after the third Test, presumably because he had taken only 5 wickets up to that point. But there is little logic in replacing such a match-winning genius, no matter how down on his luck and out of form he is, unless there is a replacement in the wings of at least comparable quality. To put this decision into perspective, in England in 1930 Grimmett had taken 29 Test wickets; against the West Indies in 1930/31 he took 33 and against South Africa in 1931/32 a further 33. In the ensuing Ashes series in England in 1934, he was to take another 25 wickets and a year later in South Africa, his haul was 43 Test wickets. By anyone's standards that is wicket-taking of the highest calibre over a prolonged period of time. Woodfull himself had pointed out at the close of 1930 that whereas

Australia might have succeeded without Bradman, the loss of Grimmett would have proved fatal. In fact Grimmett took 40 per cent of all Test wickets taken by Australia in 1930, and yet just two years later, when he was most needed, he was dropped.

During the 1930s and for some years afterwards, there were a number of occasions and incidents when religious bias appeared to influence selections for the Australian side such as Catholics versus Protestants and Freemasons. It may be that this was the reason for Grimmett being dropped and certainly one must question the thinking processes involved because logic alone does not explain his exclusion.

Indeed the constant shuffling around of players by the Australian selectors to produce the right result saw a total of 19 players used during the Series. Asked about the dropping of Grimmett, Harold Larwood admitted the tourists were amazed and relieved because, as he put it:

> Grimmett on his day was a genius, and dropping him would have been like dropping Bradman because he'd made a couple of ducks. He'd taken a pile of wickets against us in 1930 and had a couple of Tests when he didn't do much, but he was clearly a class act. We thought it was lunacy but we were quite happy about it.

And some sort of madness it does seem to have been because Grimmett and O'Reilly in tandem and in form would have been a most formidable pair.

Immediately after being discarded following the third Test, Grimmett travelled to Brisbane with the South Australia team for their Shield match against Queensland. He took 13 wickets. Whether it was because of the influence of Bradman is speculation, but it is a fact that Grimmett never again played for Australia after the Don became captain. He was totally ignored for the 1936/37 Ashes series and was then omitted from the touring party to England in 1938, a decision that Bill O'Reilly condemned as "sheer madness". Grimmett's leg-spinning replacement on that tour was Frank Ward, whose career Test record was 11 wickets at an average of 52. One excuse was that Grimmett was too old, but that had not prevented Bert Ironmonger being picked at the age of 48. Grimmett was a couple of years younger.

Was this due to religious prejudice? Grimmett (who, in any event, was a New Zealander) had been brought up in a Catholic family, his mother Mary having been born in County Roscommon, Ireland. He later became disenchanted with the Catholic Church, but both Fingleton and O'Reilly have stated that religious prejudice played a large part in the selectors' decisions, particularly anti-Catholic sentiment. Bradman had been inducted into Freemasonry at the age of 21 and was to continue as an ardent Mason all his life. The degree of discrimination is perhaps difficult to understand in England where, for the most part, difference of religion plays little if any part, and certainly not in cricket, but there is a far larger Catholic community in Australia. Even as late as the mid-1950s, a Sydney secretarial applicant would be told: "I'm sorry, we don't employ Catholics" and it was not until the late 1960s that one of Australia's largest department stores dropped a 'Protestants Only' employment policy.

Australia's most successful Test off-spinner, Ashley Mallett, described Grimmett in 1993 as "The Bradman of Spin", an accolade obviously not bestowed lightly. Yet Grimmett was discarded in what appears to have been muddled thinking and, maybe, prejudice on the part of the Australian selectors.

However there was one very talented young spinner who was making a name for himself – Fleetwood-Smith, an unconventional left-handed chinaman and googly bowler. In the previous season he had taken 37 wickets at an average of 16 and during the 1932/33 season he was to take 50 wickets at 22. Prior to the start of the Test series he had played one match for Victoria against MCC in November when Hammond decided to take him on and made 203 out of an MCC total of 408 for 9 declared, Fleetwood-Smith's analysis being 2 for 124. In his autobiography *Long Innings* Warner wrote that the MCC feared the potential of Fleetwood-Smith and Hammond had been persuaded to hit him out of contention, which apparently he did. Warner says they all rejoiced at his non-selection because 'he certainly bowled a very difficult ball.'

Had the Australian selectors missed another trick? Or were they, as Arthur Mailey says, merely looking at scoreboards?

Talking about this omission Harold Larwood could only say that he had never faced Fleetwood-Smith himself, but he recalled there had been some talk about him being a potential danger man. However Larwood agreed with Warner that the feeling in the English team was that they were better off not having to deal with his unusual style of bowling.

The Australian selectors for the 1932/33 series were Dr Charles Dolling, Chappie Dwyer and William Johnson, representing South Australia, New South Wales and Victoria respectively. Whilst the basis for their being put forward by their States as national selectors is not clear, the panel did have a distinct lack of first-class experience. In total the three of them had between them played in only 33 first-class matches and none had been a Test player. Considering that these men were national selectors, not merely State selectors, the dearth of personal experience does seem strange and may have played a part in the puzzling selection decisions. Also one must wonder if the fact that they represented only three States brought State favouritism into the choices of the individuals concerned.

By comparison, the English selectors for the tour, Lord Hawke, Peter Perrin, TA Higson and Warner, had over 1,700 matches behind them, and although Higson was mainly a businessman, he had played for Derbyshire, Lancashire and Oxford University. One should take into account that more County matches were played than in the Sheffield Shield but nonetheless the difference is still remarkable. On top of this experience in the England selection committee, there was Jardine himself, who by then had played in over 200 first-class matches, plus 11 Tests. However, even this experienced band decided to leave out Hendren for the 1932/33 tour who was to average nearly 50 in the ensuing 1934 Ashes series. Perhaps they thought him too old for an arduous tour at the age of 43.

Choosing the teams for the preceding series against West Indies in 1930/31 and South Africa in 1931/32 would have presented the Australian selectors with little in the way of problems, because Australia had won 9 of the 10 Test matches played and in those two seasons Bradman had scored 1,253 Test runs at an average of 125.30. The selectors would have been under no pressure to seek new talent mid-series during those matches, and because of the successful Test results they would have had no reason to use any fresh initiatives.

The question must be asked, therefore, whether this group was really up to the difficult tasks with which they were faced? Also, bearing in mind the problems of communication and travel over considerable distances at that time, having one selector based in Adelaide, another in Melbourne and the third in Sydney would have made effective and efficient discussion, comparing of notes and so on, extremely difficult. It would not have been easy in the best of circumstances, but in the face of a crisis requiring new and quick decisions, it would have been very difficult.

However, if MCC could be autocratic towards the professionals, the Australian Board of Control was equally dictatorial and unreasonable. Arthur Mailey, a leg-spinner whose Test record of 86 wickets in the Ashes series between 1920 and 1926 speaks for itself, was unceremoniously discarded by the Board in 1928 for the trifling sin of publishing a small article prior to receiving their permission to do so. He did actually make an approach, but the Board dismissed his request as being too late and out he went. Between them, he and Grimmett had taken 70 per cent of all Australia's wickets in 1926, and his bowling was sadly missed in the 1928/29 Series that England won 4-1. He continued playing first-class cricket up to the 1929/30 season, but was never again selected for his country. Harold Larwood commented on Mailey thus: "We'd faced Mailey in 1926 and knew just how good he was." Although by 1932 he would have been 46 years of age, one can only speculate what an experienced bowler like Mailey might have added to an Australian attack that was thin in the extreme. Moreover, even at 46 years of age, he would still have been five years younger than Ironmonger, who appeared in four of the Tests. Unlike fast bowlers, a wily spin-bowler of maturity can be a very potent weapon.

The members of the Australian Board of Control were all esteemed business and professional men, but, as Jack Fingleton described in his book *Cricket Crisis*, their predominant feature was the absence amongst their number of people who had played a decent standard of cricket. Fingleton went on to say that, considering the Board was in supreme control of the game in Australia, it was surely a most amazing state of affairs that only four legislators of international standard had found seats on the Board since its formation in 1905. In 1932, only two, from the State of Queensland, had even played Sheffield Shield. It may have been this paucity of actual cricket experience that had led to the situation described by Mailey whereby the scoreboard appeared to have been the only selection criterion, for if hardly anyone on the Board had played first-class cricket, what other basis did they have for their opinions? It might also be added that Fingleton made his remarks after he had retired from the game and by then had no reason to fear the same sort of retribution the Board had inflicted on Arthur Mailey.

Australia at that time did possess bowlers who were reasonably fast – 'Bull' Alexander, Laurie Nash, Ron Halcombe, Eddie Gilbert, for instance – but seemingly no bowlers who were both fast AND accurate. The word 'seemingly' has been used here deliberately. If, as Jack Fingleton has written, the Australian Board of Control was made up of prominent business and professional dignitaries and almost totally lacking in first-class cricket experience, then where was the knowledge or the perception to recognise talent that had yet to appear on Arthur Mailey's scoreboard? Presumably this Board was responsible for appointing the National Selectors. Is it possible that the talent so badly needed did exist, but had either been cast adrift as in the case of Mailey, or was not recognised because it had yet to appear on a scoreboard? Since then Australia has been very adept, from time to time, at producing a rabbit from the hat, that is a player hardly heard of for Test cricket, but that sort of trick was not likely to be performed by Cricket Board members almost devoid of actual cricket experience.

'Bull' Alexander, a Victorian, was certainly fast-ish but in seven years of Sheffield Shield cricket he took 95 wickets at an average of 34. His bowling may at times have been dramatic but 13 wickets a season hardly indicates bowling of the highest class and although he may have possessed speed, the accuracy was not there. Laurie Nash, also from Victoria, had been selected for just one Test, against South Africa in 1931/32, and not again until 1936/37, when he was once more picked for one Test against England. In that Test he had match figures of 5 for 104 but was then dropped and never again selected. His overall Test bowling average was only 12.59 and his first class average, 28.33. He had taken 3 for 39 in the MCC first innings in November 1932, but apparently that was not good enough. This was the same match where Nagel had taken 8 for 32. Another bowler of some speed was Ron Halcombe, from South Australia, but in a career of 25 first-class matches, he took only 54 wickets at an average of 38, so it seems his accuracy, or rather lack of it, would have told against him at Test level. In the 1932/33 season his first class wicket haul appears to have been only five, also his action seems to have been suspect, but this issue had not prevented the Australian Selectors from persisting with Ironmonger.

And then there was Eddie Gilbert. If the English selectors allowed class considerations to hamper England's prospects, in Australia, other than religion, the bias seems to have been one of racial prejudice. The discrimination was not as widespread as the class attitudes in England, but in Gilbert, Australia had the fastest bowler in the country by far. Gilbert was Aborigine however and it seems to have been nothing other than colour prejudice and racial bigotry that kept him from the Test scene and right at a time when Australia was crying out for some sheer, raw pace. Not for nothing was Gilbert called 'The Black Streak'. He was then aged 27 and in 23 matches for Queensland he took 87 wickets at an average of 28. Such was the attitude to Gilbert that although he played for Queensland for five seasons between 1930 and 1935 one Queensland player refused to even speak to him, one batsman deliberately tried to run him out in his first game, and others refused to share train sleeping compartments, hotel rooms, taxis, or even dining tables with him. Gilbert was not tall, about 170cm, roughly the same height as the 1950s West Indian fast bowler, Roy Gilchrist. Like Gilchrist, he had very long arms, but Gilbert was a quiet, well-spoken and modest personality compared with the volatile Gilchrist. He could generate tremendous pace off a short run-up of just a few paces and this was seized by racists as proof that his action had to be illegal. "Nobody could bowl that fast off such a short run without chucking" it was said. Like Larwood his short stature meant that his trajectory was lower and thus he was faster off the pitch. Allegations of an illegal action had never prevented Australia from selecting Ironmonger so these accusations appear to have been aimed solely at discrediting Gilbert, rather than being based on fact. In any case, he was still playing in 1935/36 and his action had not changed.

The inability of the Australian cricket establishment to accept the success of an Aborigine was not without precedent, for a similar fate had befallen Aboriginal fast bowler Jack Marsh in 1901. Marsh was also extremely quick but, despite taking 34 wickets at an average of 21 in only six matches for New South Wales, he was removed by a similar orchestrated plot. In what appears to have been a deliberate attempt to remove this embarrassment by discrediting him, he was no-balled seventeen times by a

Victorian umpire. This was, of course, the precise excuse the racial knockers were seeking in order to argue that he could not be selected. In his book *Farewell to Cricket*, Bradman said that the fastest six balls he had ever faced were those bowled by Gilbert in November 1931 - only six, because the sixth ball had dismissed Bradman. Ball number five was so fast that it completely knocked Bradman's bat from his hands. By comparison it is interesting to note that when Larwood knocked Woodfull's bat from his hands in 1932, the local press claimed it was proof of brutal bowling. According to Gilbert's biographers Mike Colman and Ken Edwards, in a later Shield match in 1936, Bradman placed himself lower down in the batting order so as to avoid Gilbert at his fastest.

In a discussion of this situation, Harold Larwood commented that Gilbert was by far the fastest bowler they encountered, but he had no idea why he was never selected. Otherwise, he said Australia didn't seem to have possessed much of an opening attack and, having disposed of Grimmett, relied very largely on their remaining spinners. "Wall was quickish," he said, "but although he got a few wickets, including five in our first innings at Adelaide, I don't think our batsmen were too worried about him. He wasn't what you'd call a Test strike bowler, which Gilbert might have been."

It seems that whilst opening bowlers of some pace may have existed in Australia at the time, few were thought to be sufficiently fast and/or accurate to be considered for a Test place. In the case of Gilbert, where they did have a bowler whose speed alone would have been a shock tactic, he was the wrong colour and had to be kept out of sight, because an Aboriginal success would have presented a cultural problem. For the rest, even had they been selected, none could have bowled leg-theory without causing expensive embarrassment in the process. Australia thus found themselves faced with a form of bowling attack that they had not thought of and which, when they did consider it, they found they could not adopt because they just did not possess the necessary equipment.

And what about the batsmen selected by Australia? Did their ages tell against them when faced with a style of attack that required quick reflexes and rapid footwork? This had not been a problem in 1930/31 or 1931/32, but the Jardine team, even without leg-theory, had faster and more accurate bowlers than anything they had had to face of late. If Australia did not have bowlers of accurate pace, as seems to have been the case, then none of their batsmen would have had any practice against real speed on Australian wickets, and the fact that they lacked the fleetness of foot or the reflexes of youth to handle it may not have been apparent. In addition to this, because of the absence of top speed, the uneven and unpredictable bounce of the Australian pitches may not have looked like much of a problem and therefore attracted little comment. However, the difficulties that this factor could present were to come into clear focus when bowlers of extreme pace appeared.

This fact was emphasised by the famed Australian Test fast bowler, Ernie Jones – a very fast bowler – when he commented in a local newspaper before the second Test that Australian batsmen lacked practice against real pace, saying 'the fault lies not with our batsmen but their lack of practice against bowlers of real speed.'

A similar opinion was voiced by Maurice Tate, who wrote:

The boot was on the other foot and our own experience of 1921, when Australia had Gregory and McDonald and we had got out of the habit of playing really fast bowling, was now forgotten.

Was one of the problems the fact that Australian batsmen had become too comfortable with the opening bowlers in Grade and Shield cricket at that time and were just not prepared for extreme speed when they had to contend with it? Woodfull was 35, Ponsford 32 and Richardson 38. After just one Test, Kippax, who was also 35, was clearly not quick enough to handle leg-theory and was dropped. He had averaged 55 with the bat in the 1930 Series, but was never again the same player at Test level. Bradman was 24, McCabe 22. Jackson, too, was in that age group but he was at the tail end of his fight with tuberculosis.

The Australian selectors appear to have shuffled their available cards in a confused manner. As an example of how they fiddled with the batting, experienced campaigner Bill Ponsford, whose career Test batting average of 48.22 speaks for itself, was selected for the first Test, dropped for the second, picked up again for the third and fourth Tests and discarded once

Bill Ponsford, a victim of the Australian selectors' indecision,
whilst in his prime.

more for the fifth. Ponsford had averaged 55.00 in the 1930 series and in 1934 his Test batting average of 94.83 was higher than that of Bradman. His career Test batting average has been bettered by only eleven Australian batsmen. Surely class enough to have warranted selector confidence. Similarly, Jack Fingleton, although then a newcomer, who was to average 42 in his full Test career, was dropped after making a pair in the third Test. He had made 150 runs in the first two Tests as against Woodfull's mere 43 and Richardson's 115. In his case he seems also to have been blamed for leaking to the press the comments made by Woodfull to Warner during the third Test that only one team was playing cricket. An allegation that was never proved. Although averaging 62 in the 1933/34 Sheffield Shield season he was omitted completely from the 1934 touring side. Like Clarrie Grimmett, Fingleton was a Catholic at a time when such matters counted and when community prejudice ruled. Was this a case where a Catholic who failed once was likely to be discarded, whereas a Protestant would be given another chance?

When talking about this with Harold Larwood, he said they were surprised that a batsman of Ponsford's quality was in and out of the side and that Len Darling had not been brought in earlier. "Darling impressed us when playing for Victoria," he said. "I wasn't playing in that match, but he looked pretty quick on his feet and he was left-handed." Darling was selected for the last two Tests of the 1932/33 series, finishing with 148 runs at an average of 37 and was third in the Australian batting averages. However, his Test performances waned thereafter, and he finished his Test career with a batting average of 27.8.

Another mystery pointed out by Harold Larwood was the absence of Allan Fairfax. In 1932 he would have been only 26. "He had looked pretty good when we saw him in the last Test of 1928/29 and he had done quite well as an all-rounder in 1930 too," said Harold. Fairfax had toured England in 1930, playing in four of the Tests, averaging 50 with the bat and taking 12 wickets at 27. He averaged 48 in five Tests against the West Indies the following season, but then apparently became so disenchanted by the atmosphere generated by Australian barracking that he left the game for good at the end of 1931/32. At the blossoming age of 26, a very useful and proven all-rounder had been lost. Chipperfield, who was picked for the ensuing 1934 tour, had made 153 against MCC towards the end of the tour in February 1933 and was batting well in Grade matches. He hadn't been picked for New South Wales against MCC, but here was a talent that seems to have been overlooked. And, at 27, he was no newcomer. Then there was Bill Brown, who had batted well for New South Wales against MCC. He was then 22 and was to go on to play in 22 Tests, split by World War II, for a career Test batting average of 46. It seems to have been out of character for Australia not to try young blood.

All in all, what emerges is a picture of confusion and strange decisions when faced with a situation for which neither the Australian Board nor the Selectors were prepared. The previous two years had been very easy for them. 1932/33 was to present a very different set of problems.

So much for the apparent confusion in the Australian Test selections, but what about Douglas Jardine himself? Let us have an unbiased look at him.

DOUGLAS JARDINE: THE MYTHS AND THE MAN

"Jardine's tenacity, courage and tactical skill have rarely been equalled by any touring captain."

Walter Hammond, 1946

"I have never played under a better tactician than D R Jardine. He takes a lot of knowing. He stays within his shell and in doing so creates, I'm afraid, a wrong impression. But I learned differently in 1932/33. Then I learned that Jardine was one of the greatest men I have met."

Herbert Sutcliffe, 1935

DOUGLAS JARDINE WAS born in 1900 in Bombay, where his father, Malcom, was a barrister, a profession he had followed on there from his own father, W J Jardine. The Jardine family were steeped in cricket, Malcolm having been in the University team at Oxford and had scored 140 in the Universities match of 1892 and three of his brothers had been in the Rugby school cricket team.

In India the family was comfortably off, but not wealthy. Douglas was sent to Norris Hill Preparatory School, near Newbury, in 1910, and then went on to Winchester in 1914, where he captained the 1st XI in his final year, with a batting average of 66. In 1919 he went up to Oxford, where he was awarded a cricket Blue and was reasonably successful, without being exceptional, in his four years there. He was not made captain in his final year, but this was partly due to sustaining a serious injury to his right knee that subsequently constrained his batting and prevented him from bowling his leg-breaks. At that time there was also an outstanding contemporary at the University by the name of Greville Stevens.

On coming down from Oxford, Jardine played for Surrey as an amateur whilst qualifying as a solicitor and was made vice-captain to Percy Fender in 1924. Thereafter he played regularly for Surrey, with the exceptions of the 1929 and 1930 seasons when, for business reasons, he could manage only nine matches. In most of the other seasons, he was usually either at the top or well up in the County Championship batting averages.

In 1928 Jardine was selected for two of the Test matches against the West Indies, averaging 52.5, and in 1928/29 was a member of Percy Chapman's Ashes side to Australia, where he played in all five Test matches, emerging with a batting average of 42.6. It was on this tour, and apparently solely because of his appearance, that Jardine came under fire from Australian barrackers, however the reason for this has never been logically explained.

Previous books on the 1932/33 tour appear to have concentrated on depicting Jardine as a difficult man, as an aloof and autocratic snob and in just about every quoted instance there is no alternative opinion or interpretation offered. Incidents, situations and statements seem to have been taken at face value, or without any attempt being made to enquire whether any other reason existed. In fact, since his death in 1958, it appears to have become popular to criticise and find fault with Jardine, without stopping to consider the possibility of other factors being involved. It is therefore interesting to speculate on why this is so.

One of the most quoted comments about Douglas Jardine was made by former Test player Rockley Wilson to a journalist on the eve of the 1932/33 tour. When asked what England's chances were under Jardine, Wilson apparently said, "He might well win us the Ashes, but we might lose a Dominion." Many writers immediately homed in on this as a criticism of Jardine – but was it? Wilson played first-class cricket from 1899 to 1923, ending with 467 wickets at an average of 17.6 runs per wicket. In addition to having been a master at Winchester when Jardine was there, he had also been a member of the 1920/21 England team to Australia and at that time was already 41

England captain Douglas Jardine replete with the infamous Harlequin cap.

years of age. He only played in the last Test at Sydney bowling his leg-breaks credibly enough to emerge with match figures of 3 for 36 in 21 overs. However, he had to endure sarcastic comments from the crowd, apparently because, due to his age, his throwing arm had gone and when fielding he had to throw in under-arm. He was also subjected to hostile spectator comments because he had written reports on the ribald barracking of Hobbs, who had a strained thigh and was therefore somewhat lame. Crowd derision aimed at a cricketer who was injured, plus his own treatment in the field, would hardly have impressed him. The question that naturally arises therefore is whether Wilson's comment was really aimed at Jardine – or was he thinking back some ten years earlier to his own experiences in Australia? The question takes on heightened relevance because Wilson made the above oft-quoted comment when Jardine's captaincy was announced, some time before the leg-theory strategy was even on the horizon. Would he have made this comment had Jardine been selected to lead a tour to, for instance, South Africa, and if not, then why Australia? Even after the

1932/33 Australian tour, Jardine led a successful MCC side to India in 1933/34, so what was the real focus of Wilson's remark? It seems possible that what Wilson may have had in mind was the atmosphere in Australia and not Jardine himself at all. Knowing Jardine well, Wilson most probably also knew that the man would calmly ignore both the inventions of the Australian press and the Australian barracker.

This raises an interesting proposition. Should the MCC have selected their captains for an Australian tour only on the basis of what their coming hosts would find acceptable? Should the MCC have refused to play unless crowds were controlled? Had they demonstrated more resolve in this respect, might this not have influenced a range of later events? It may be said that visiting cricket teams must put up with the local cultural environment and, whilst this may be true to some extent, unprovoked crowd hostility is surely an aspect that could have been examined, with certain criteria demanded as a pre-tour condition. Difficult to achieve, maybe, but if the Australian authorities had been put on notice, it might have made a considerable difference. Compare this problem with crowd behaviour in England, where such hostilities were almost unknown at that time and even now are relatively quiet compared with Australia.

There have been numerous published comments on Jardine from members of the English team, but to a large extent they appear to have been ignored or the player's views have been disparaged on the basis that the books were 'only ghosted'. Ghosting is a means whereby an experienced and fluent style can improve the writing, but in no way does it imply the recollections or opinions expressed are not the fundamental views of the player under whose name the book is published. Perhaps this is just another example of the apparent tendency to ignore anything that was pro-Jardine, because all members of his team were very supportive of him.

Let us have a look at their published comments:

Walter Hammond

As a central figure of the team, and one of England's greatest cricketers, it seems strange that Hammond's comments have largely been ignored. In his book *Cricket My Destiny*, published in 1946, Hammond wrote:

In a little book, *The Barracker at Bay*, which I believe attained considerable popularity and success in Australia after the end of our 1932/33 tour, there is a passage which I believe throws a crucial light on the bodyline rumpus. It runs: "When the news reached us of Jardine's appointment as captain, Australians generally had misgivings. Although only a private in Chapman's band of 1928, Jardine had attracted a certain amount of unfavourable comment because of his apparent aloofness and superciliousness. When a member of the rank and file is remembered after four years there must be some reason."

Anyone who has ever played in a team with Douglas Jardine has been struck by his imperturbability, his calmness when things go wrong, and equally when they go right, his cold determination to win, neither giving nor seeking quarter.

The Australians themselves have admitted many times that they do not like such an attitude – though among their cricket captains of recent years is more than one who displays similar characteristics. But, when a visitor to Australia is like that, the crowds imagine he is "giving them the Colonial" – trying to adopt a superior air, because he comes from the Old Country. In Jardine's case, nothing of the sort could have been intended, because he treats everyone, Australians and his own team, distinguished patrons of the game and autograph-hunters, in exactly the same way.

Hammond went on to say:

But there is no doubt that many of the barrackers resented Jardine more than Larwood. Of all cricketers, Jardine is perhaps the last who would deliberately infringe a rule, so the yells of the crowd in his case arose from something other than resentment at supposed unfairness. They had it waiting for him, I think, before he set foot in Australia at all. Yet I shall always feel that he was the best skipper we could have had, if the MCC wanted to get the Ashes back again, for his tenacity, courage and tactical skill have rarely been equalled by any touring captain.

It is strange that these published comments from Walter Hammond hardly seem to have been noticed, but coming from a cricketer of his stature, they must have some import. What has been mentioned is the comment supposedly made by Hammond, privately, that he detested leg-theory and had done so during the tour. However, without any evidence identifying when or where or whoever is supposed to have heard this comment, it remains nothing more than hearsay.

The Australian press' portrayal of Jardine's attitude does not appear to have carried any weight in New Zealand. The controversies of the 1932/33 tour were reported in detail, so New Zealand was well aware of what had gone before when England went on to that country at the end of their Australian tour and much to the annoyance of the Australians, for some strange reason. Like Australia, New Zealand in the early 1930s regarded itself as a frontier country, and it might have been expected there would be a similar reaction to Jardine's appearance and so-called attitude. It is probably true to say that New Zealand is culturally closer to Australia than any other Commonwealth country, and the fact that nothing in Jardine's clothing, demeanour, etc., caused any adverse comment there is interesting. It does seem to suggest a problem of Australian attitude rather than something for which Jardine could be criticised. Australians complained about what they perceived as Jardine's "apparent aloofness and supercilious-ness", but even though forewarned, the New Zealanders seemed to have found nothing in Jardine to dislike at all, despite there being no change in his dress or conduct. After all, if it was merely Jardine's mien and turnout, then why did these not provoke the same reaction in New Zealand? In actual fact the English team commented on how enjoyable it was to play cricket in New Zealand, in pleasant surroundings and devoid of hooting spectators.

Anger at a perceived attitude and derision of his colourful Harlequin cap seems to have been an Australian problem, for nowhere else had Jardine encountered such a reaction. He never went as a cricketer to South Africa, but taking New Zealand as a reasonable rule of thumb, it is unlikely he would have encountered the same reception in South Africa as in Australia. There was no leg-theory during the 1928/29 tour to Australia when Jardine was pilloried. He was just an ordinary member of the side, but he was booed and sneered at simply because of his appearance and imagined demeanour. Yet these were no different from when he was playing cricket in England, and there had never been any comment there. As Harold Larwood said in his book *Bodyline?* and confirmed to this author, in his view and experience there were (perhaps still are) two Australias - one inside the cricket grounds and the other, the real Australia, outside. Jack Hobbs said the same thing. It seems that Douglas Jardine could behave, dress and appear just as he liked on any cricket field, anywhere in the world - except in Australia. An element of the Australian cricket crowds seemed to have some need to mock and ridicule English players and fielders in particular. They would have been frustrated in their efforts and in their attempts at humour as far as Jardine was concerned, because he simply ignored them and this attitude no doubt enraged and irritated them even further.

Herbert Sutcliffe

If Hammond was a central figure on that tour, then equally so was Sutcliffe. He had formed with Jack Hobbs one of the most famous and successful Test opening partnerships in the history of the game and, at the age of 38, was the senior professional. Yet his views appear to have gone unnoticed. In his book *For England And Yorkshire*, published in 1935, he wrote the following of Jardine:

> I have never played under a better tactician than D R Jardine, who captained England in Australia in 1932/33, and I have never played under a better fighter than D R Jardine. His method of studying the game set every member of his side on similar lines, and his fighting power was a wonderful source of inspiration to us all. We missed him last season, as every cricket enthusiast in the country knows, as every cricket enthusiast in Australia knows, and as every man who played with him in Australia knows. Our hearts would have been gladdened to see him on the field, instead of in the Press box. Jardine has the two vital qualifications for captaincy - he had method and personality.

In making these comments regarding Jardine's leadership Sutcliffe was placing him in a wide perspective of Test cricket captains under whom he had played since his debut in County cricket in 1919 - Gilligan, Chapman, Wyatt, Walters, Mann – not to mention a number of very shrewd Yorkshire skippers. Moreover, given Sutcliffe's experience and success as a Test cricketer, and very few can claim a career Test batting average of over 60, it may reasonably be assumed his accolade was not lightly bestowed. However, in his book, Sutcliffe also goes on to say about Jardine:

> He takes a lot of knowing. He stays within his shell and in doing so creates, I'm afraid, a wrong impression. There is an old saying that you have to live with a man to know him really well, but Jardine disproved that completely on the 1928/29 tour. Did I get to know Jardine? Not one scrap. I thought he was a queer devil.
>
> But I learned differently in 1932/33. Then I learned that Jardine was one of the greatest men I have met, a stern master, but every inch a man and as straight as they make 'em. Jardine had the courage of his convictions; it was unfortunate for him that they did not meet with general approval, but that did not alter his outlook. He planned for us, he cared for us, he fought for us on that tour, and he was so faithful in everything he did that we were prepared on our part to do anything we could for him. A great cricket captain.

Hedley Verity

Writing to Hedley Verity's father on their return to England, Jardine wrote: 'On and off the field Hedley has been a real friend and a grand help to me - you must be a very proud father and with good reason.' This was hardly the sort of relationship that would have been expected of an aloof amateur with one of his professionals and it was borne out by Verity himself in his book *Bowling 'Em Out* where he writes of the privilege of being in Australia with Jardine. In his biography of Verity *Portrait of a Cricketer* Alan Hill says that it was a friendship brimming with mutual respect, and Verity never deviated from his view that Jardine was unequalled as a captain. Verity named his second son after Douglas Jardine.

Bill Bowes

Bowes said: "DRJ was a man any father would accept as a model for his son. To me and every member of the 1932/33 MCC side in Australia Douglas Jardine was the greatest captain England ever had. A great fighter, a grand friend and an unforgiving enemy."

More recently, a supporting opinion emerged from the Australian side when Australian Test batsman Bill Brown celebrated his 94th birthday in August 2006. Interviewed by the *Sydney Morning Herald* to mark the occasion, he said he had met Douglas Jardine several times after that tour and remarked how he and mutual friends agreed Jardine was "a most charming fellow". "Bodyline," said Brown, "was his idea and he wanted to see it work. I saw him away from cricket and he was a very nice fellow, very nice." Brown did not play in any of the 1932/33 Tests, but did play in the match between MCC and New South Wales in January 1933, where he outshone his opening partner Jack Fingleton and Bradman too for that matter, making 69 and 25. Interestingly, the most successful MCC bowler was Hammond, with match figures of 9 for 65. Another view from the Australian side that appears to have been ignored is that of Arthur Mailey, who wrote that Jardine "was a colourful personality, possessing courage by the ton and a very fine sense of humour." These views do not seem to accord with the usual Australian depiction.

It may be that those who have sought to portray Jardine in a negative light did so because this assists in justifying the outcry against leg-theory. For instance, Australian cricket writer Jack McHarg, author of the 1987 biography, *Stan McCabe: The man and his cricket*, says that Jardine had decided four years prior to the 1932/33 tour that he didn't like Australians. There is no evidence to support this contention, although Jardine was unlikely to have been impressed by the comments of the Australian barracker. On the other hand, there is plenty of evidence that four years earlier some Australians had decided, for whatever reason, that they didn't like Douglas Jardine. McHarg has reversed the respective roles here to give colour to his allegation and remove any responsibility from Australia. Of course, it is possible he may have hoped that the barracking in 1928/29 had in fact produced his claimed reaction in Jardine.

Harold Larwood's recollections on the question of Jardine's attitude towards Australians in general are illuminating. Probed on this issue from various angles, Harold was quite adamant that he never heard Jardine say anything or saw any action that gave the impression Jardine disliked Australians in general, although he didn't think much of the barrackers. Nor did he ever hear Jardine even mention the treatment Harold had seen him receive from Australian crowds when they were in the same team in 1928/29. Certainly, he said, there were tactical discussions, but these were cool and thought out in depth and never was there anything nasty, vicious or personal in Jardine's language when talking about Bradman or anyone else in the Australian team. "We had heard rumours from somewhere, probably some local newspaper," said Harold, "that Mr Jardine always referred to Bradman as 'the little bastard'. Mr Jardine was not that sort of person. As far as I can remember, I only ever heard him use that expression on one occasion and that was during the last Test when I wanted to go off the field and he wanted me to stay to maintain some psychological pressure on Bradman." Larwood said Jardine had many friends in Australia, as was demonstrated by the numerous social invitations he received and the many he accepted. Why then was he depicted as an Aussie-hater by the local press? Was it simply because he ignored the barrackers? "Just because he was not all over you, hail-fellow-well-met," said Harold, "didn't mean at all that he didn't like you."

Turning to McHarg again, in the same book on McCabe, he stated that because of Jardine's austere personality, team gatherings on the voyage out had an atmosphere 'like a dentist's waiting room'. Asked about this allegation, Harold Larwood said it was total nonsense. He said that team gatherings although frequently involving tactical discussions where any suggestions were welcomed by Jardine, were always informal and enthusiastic. Moreover, he said, the 1932/33 touring party had wonderful team spirit throughout. This view is confirmed by Plum Warner in *The Book of Cricket* where he writes:

During a time of storm and stress and in a very tense atmosphere, no body of men could have behaved better and with more loyalty, discretion and good temper, and sound sense than this MCC side.

Other writers have said that Jardine kept himself aloof from the rest of the team on the voyage out. Harold said, "He was no different from Mr Chapman on the voyage out for the 1928/29 series. Amateurs did tend to keep their own company in those days, but the overall atmosphere of that 1932/33 voyage was friendly and enjoyable." This description appears to be confirmed by Plum Warner in his book *Cricket Between Two Wars* in which he described the atmosphere on the Orontes as 'convivial'. If, because of Jardine, the atmosphere within the team was indeed as cold and forbidding as some have attempted to make out, it seems odd that a cricketer of the standing of Herbert Sutcliffe should have written the glowing testimony already quoted. Overlooked, too, is the fact that on the voyage from Canada back to the UK at the end of the tour, the entire team clubbed together to present Jardine with a silver cigar box, engraved with all their autographs. The inscription read:

> In appreciation and admiration of his
> leadership and wonderful courage.

There is no record of a similar gesture to either of Jardine's Ashes touring predecessors - Gilligan or Chapman, nor to Allen nor indeed any other Ashes captain. This gift was a demonstration of team loyalty and affection and it speaks for itself but for some odd reason it has hardly been mentioned elsewhere. Of this unique gesture, Jack Hobbs wrote:

> A great skipper and a great fighter! A man thoroughly deserving the splendid present, with the splendid inscription, given to him by his men on the way home. No wonder the fellows he led were proud of Jardine.

Much has been made of Jardine's Harlequin cap and the fact that this was the cause for much of the barracking. The Harlequins are an Oxford cricket club dating from 1852. The rules specify that there should be no more than 20 resident members, and new members are elected on the recommendation of the current University captain. Membership, for which there is no entrance fee or subscription, is for life. According to cricket author David Frith, Australian writer and historian Manning Clark was a Harlequin member and said that there was nothing very unusual about it. That being the case, and here we have the opinion of an Australian, then just what was all the fuss about? It may be a colourful cap, but so are the caps of I Zingari, MCC, Free Foresters, Stragglers of Asia, and so on. Did this mean that you wore anything even slightly out of the ordinary in Australia at your peril? To quote Donald Horne once more: 'To appear ordinary, just like everybody else, is sometimes a necessary condition for success in Australia.' Was this one of the reasons?

Several authors have quoted situations where they say Jardine's attitude or response is proof that he was an aloof, Australian-hating snob. Whilst it is not claimed that the views of Harold Larwood are necessarily to be taken as definitive on this subject, he did get to know Jardine well on that tour. His views as an ex-professional cricketer, expressed many years later and apparently never before canvassed, perhaps do carry some weight. One situation, much quoted, is where Jardine, along with a couple of other members of the team, were accosted in a friendly fashion at a railway station by some fellow who recognised them as members of the England side. The story goes that the other two players were happy enough to respond to this spontaneous approach, but Jardine merely stared at the man, seemingly perplexed. When relayed to Harold Larwood, he responded that coming from a formal social background – the Raj in India – where it was expected that people would be introduced rather than merely walk up and start talking, Jardine would probably have simply been nonplussed by the situation. No excuse, it might be said, but it does provide an explanation that does not appear to have been considered before.

In 1983 Lawrence Le Quesne's book *The Bodyline Controversy* was published and just a year later *Douglas Jardine – Spartan Cricketer* by Christopher Douglas appeared. It is puzzling that the two books contained such conflicting portrayals of Jardine. Le Quesne seemed to produce an image of a man who was austere, aloof, patronising, humourless and an Australian-hating disciplinarian. He says that Jardine regarded both Australian crowds and the press with contempt. Certainly Jardine ignored the barrackers so what else would have been expected of him and given the inventions of the press, he could hardly have been expected to bring them

Jardine leads his England side onto the field for the second Test at Melbourne.

into his confidence! Enough exaggerations had already appeared without him actually inviting more. Yet Le Quesne seems to feel that Jardine should have adopted an appeasing strategy and tried to make himself popular and by contrast, the appraisal produced by Christopher Douglas portrays quite a different personality. It seems strange that this sort of comment should have been made in a book published in 1983, when only four years earlier, Mike Brearley had encountered exactly the same reaction from Australian barrackers as Jardine had received. Brearley had tried the friendly wave, the response that Le Quesne says Jardine should have adopted, and the only thanks Brearley got for his gesture was to have even more beer cans launched at him.

To go back even further to see the futility of attempting reason with the Australian barracker, one might consider the treatment handed out to Percy Chapman in 1929. It is generally accepted that Chapman was a reasonably engaging and extrovert character, described by Swanton as "gay and ever boyish", (who also sometimes wore a Harlequin cap) so one would

The scene at the Adelaide Oval during the third Test in which the mood of the patrons against Jardine's continued use of 'bodyline' grew close revolt.

think that these attributes would have endeared him to the crowds. However, a barracking furore exploded in Melbourne when Chapman brought on Larwood to bowl at a tail-end batsman, Ironmonger. Despite Chapman actively trying to reason with the crowd, the booing, hissing and general abuse were only brought to a halt by the Victorian captain, Ryder, who declared their innings closed. Chapman was so insulted and jostled at Melbourne, even in the Members enclosure, that this may well have been his reason for leaving himself out of the final Test. Bradman was just emerging, having played in four of those Tests for a batting average of 66, and leg-theory was not even a dot on the horizon, but Chapman had won the first four Tests and this may have been an influential factor in the crowds behaviour. As Jack Hobbs was to observe: "Sometimes the Australian club members joined in the barracking, and I thought that was discreditable". With that sort of trail to follow, what hope did Jardine have? It should be pointed out that not even Jardine was ever physically abused and moreover, why did MCC do nothing about this level of misbehaviour by the Australian crowd and Members when Chapman presumably reported it on his return to England?

To consider Le Quesne again, he describes Douglas Jardine as having a 'stiff, crane-like, contemptuous bearing, his silk choker and his Harlequin cap, the model of overbearing English arrogance.' Harold Larwood had not read Le Quesne's book, but when this passage was shown to him, his reaction was one of amazement. "You know," he said, "the trouble is that some people will believe tripe like that, and it is so far from the truth. Anyway, just what is stiff and crane-like supposed to mean? Was it a crime to be tall and slim? And he wasn't that stiff in the field I can tell you! Mr Jardine was a very good catcher." The choker was worn by other amateurs on that tour, such as Brown and Pataudi, and was common for amateurs at that time. Ames wore one on occasions. As a sweat-soaker, it was probably cotton, anyway. Even thirty-five years later, when it might have been thought the choker would have gone out of fashion, Hampshire captain Colin Ingleby-McKenzie was still sporting one and nobody in his right mind would have described that man as either a snob or aloof. In World War II a white silk scarf or cravat was regarded as a good luck charm and was worn by many pilots and flight crew, whether officers or not. This was really nothing more than superstition, but was regarded as neither affectation nor a form of social pretence.

Le Quesne also states that Jardine showed an extreme lack of sensitivity when he said "Well bowled" to Harold Larwood immediately following the ball that struck Woodfull during the Adelaide Test. The apparent implication being that Jardine was congratulating Larwood because he had injured Woodfull. In his book *Bodyline Autopsy* David Frith says the comment was made for the benefit of Bradman, who was batting at the other end. There is no evidence to support this tale, and in any event Bradman, as the non-striker, would obviously have been standing fairly close to Larwood, anyway, so he could hardly not have heard what was said. As is so often the case there is a different and quite logical interpretation and this is provided by Jack Hobbs in his book *The Fight for the Ashes*. Hobbs says:

The facts are that Harold opened the attack, as usual, with a few overs of normal bowling. Woodfull was struck by the last ball of the second over. Uproar sufficient to shatter the nerve of any bowler broke out from the crowd. So that Larwood should not get rattled, and for no other reason at all, Jardine said to him, "Well bowled, Harold". When Woodfull recovered from his injury, there was an over from the other end, and then, following his usual practice, Jardine switched his field to leg-theory. Facts, as you see, have a knack of changing rumours.

Asked why he thought Jardine had said this, Larwood merely confirmed Hobbs' view of the situation. "What he was doing," said Harold, "was simply to reassure me that it was an accident, and that I should not let it upset me or allow myself to be put off either by what had happened or the noise of the crowd, that's all. And the switch to leg-theory was planned at that time anyway, because the ball was no longer swinging away. That ball just got up because of unpredictable bounce and it wasn't pitched anywhere near leg stump." What might the reaction have been had the boot been on the other foot? There have been several Australian captains of recent years who would not have shrunk from the move if it were already on the cards. For instance, can one imagine Ian Chappell saying to either Lillee or Thomson, 'We'd better go easy on these blokes as you seem to have injured a couple of them'? Some years after Jardine maybe, but having complained so bitterly about Larwood in 1932/33 it does put such events into context.

A similar situation seems to have occurred with Gilbert Mant, who had been the Reuters reporter in 1932/33. Mant waited 60 years before writing his book *A Cuckoo in the Bodyline Nest*. He says he introduced himself to Jardine on the ship carrying the team to Australia. According to Mant, and there were no witnesses, Jardine, who was reading a book in a deckchair at the time, merely responded with the words, "I see". This reply, if true, certainly appears a little brusque, but this fleeting incident appears to have festered in Mant's mind over the ensuing years, for one chapter in his book carries the dramatic title of *The Unspeakable Jardine*. Mant claims this title meant only that Jardine did not speak to him, but from the obvious double meaning of the word, it seems clear he felt it to have been a deliberate snub.

As Harold Larwood has said, Jardine expected people to be introduced by others rather than introduce themselves. Old-fashioned if you like, but not necessarily a calculated slight. And, was this also the innate shyness that Harold Larwood described? In answer to Oldfield's advice to ignore the crowd, Jardine is alleged to have said that all Australians were an uncouth mob anyway, or words to that effect. Discussing this story, which he said they'd all heard, Harold Larwood merely chuckled and said: "You know, he had the driest sense of humour. He could say summat, with a perfectly straight face, and you'd not realise until some moments later the humour in what he'd just said. I don't think Mr Jardine was being deliberately offensive. It was probably just a throw-away line, indicating that they didn't worry him." Jardine's manner of speech was described by one author as 'strangulated upper-class vowels'. Prior to this comment Harold had been asked what sort of voice Jardine had and how he spoke. His answer was that he was no different in this than Allen, Warner, Wyatt or most other amateurs: "They all spoke the same way," he said.

A number of authors have also referred to Jardine's 'nefarious venture' or 'being bent on vengeance', and as 'a dedicated and implacable avenger', as if this were some vicious personal vendetta. Vengeance for what, one may ask? The last time Jardine had faced the Australians was on the victorious 1928/29 tour, in which he finished with a batting average of 41. He had played very little cricket during the 1930 English season and appeared in none of the Tests that year, so just what axe is it imagined he had to grind? In his book *Ashes in the Mouth*, Ronald Mason comments that despite the belligerence and declared intention to cause bodily harm of Messrs Lillee and Thomson (at which they succeeded and caused far more injuries than Larwood ever did), 'they did not have at their backs the same kind of determined policy that Jardine conceived'. 'A determined and ruthless tactician' is the way Mason describes Jardine. Mr Mason seems to have known little about Ian Chappell, because if ever there was an Australian captain who did have determined policy and was totally ruthless in using all weapons at his disposal, including sledging, it was surely Chappell. Yet, as in other cases, it seems that it is only Jardine who was at fault. It is because of such wishful Corinthianisms that many Australians understandably regard a large proportion of the English as amusing fossils.

After the third Test Jardine did in fact call a team meeting and asked them all if, following the Adelaide fracas, they felt that leg-theory should be discarded as a tactic. Harold Larwood said the team was unanimous in saying they could see no reason to change anything. "You will all have a much happier tour if I did," Jardine said. According to Bill Bowes, the comment from Maurice Leyland almost in disbelief, was "What, give up leg-theory just because it's got 'em licked?" Harold Larwood was asked, "What about Allen – what did he say in view of his refusal to bowl leg-theory?" Harold said he couldn't recall Allen making any comment whatsoever at the meeting. "If he had said anything I'd have remembered it," he said. "He just kept quiet."

In his study of Douglas Jardine, John Ward states that although Jardine captained the Winchester XI in his final two years, his own housethought him 'too authoritarian and intolerant', although the source for this is not clear. Had the positions been the other way round, i.e. had Jardine captained his house but was not thought good enough to captain the school, then some sort of comment might have been in perspective. However, if the school itself selected him as captain then the house captaincy does appear to have been a matter of personal choice, as against simple ability. Similarly, Swanton says of Jardine's Oxford days that the sole reason he was not appointed captain was because nobody could break through 'a certain sardonic reserve'. There were, in fact, a whole host of reasons - a leg injury, other more senior contemporaries and, in his final year, he was in the shadow of the brilliant all-rounder at Oxford, Greville Stevens, who had demonstrated such talent that he was chosen for the Gentleman whilst still a schoolboy. Arthur Gilligan, Percy Chapman and Gubby Allen were all at Cambridge, but none was ever captain. Considering the fact that all three captained England either side of Jardine, is it not strange that none of them captained their University? The same comment holds true for Peter May at Cambridge, and Freddie Brown and Colin Cowdrey at Oxford. So, once more, why single out Douglas Jardine? What were the reasons for the universities not selecting any of them?

It seems that just about every author is keen to find some aspect for criticism and inaccuracies tend to creep in. In his otherwise authoritative biography *Plum Warner* Gerald Howat states that Woodfull was hit on the head by Larwood. This is not what happened as he was struck on the chest. Howat may have made a genuine mistake, but of course being hit on the head does sound rather more dramatic. In similar fashion Howat quotes

Fingleton as saying that the match at Sydney where Fingleton made 199 not out – November 25/29 1932 – 'brought bodyline in earnest'. It is an interesting comment because in that match Allen took 7 wickets, Voce 5, Tate 4 and Brown 2. Larwood was not even playing.

On the Australian cricket website *334notout*, Jardine is described as being 'thin-faced and hook-nosed' when he went up to Oxford; such features themselves apparently justify immediate suspicion and condemnation. It is a very strange comment. Others have said that Jardine was quite unpredictable and moody, easy-going one moment, quite the opposite a moment later. Questioned on this, Harold Larwood said he had never noticed this, and he had many conversations with Jardine, some initiated by Jardine and some by Larwood himself. He said he surely would have either remarked upon it or heard some comment from another member of the team if it had been a feature of the Jardine persona. "Anyway," he said, "if he did seem somewhat preoccupied at times, he had a lot on his plate, and it was perhaps only natural, considering the enormous pressure he must have been under".

Although Australia has mellowed and matured considerably in the intervening 70 years, a stream of new Bradman literature regularly appears, and the anti-Jardine strain also continues. In 2003 the *Sydney Morning Herald* published an article on the 1932/33 series where Jardine was described as a 'psychopath', i.e. someone with a chronic mental disorder who behaves violently. It would be interesting to know how Clive Lloyd would react to being labelled a psychopath because of his non-stop fast bowling line-up. His successful strategy of a brutal barrage of bouncers and consistent, searing, lifting pace caused far more injuries than leg-theory ever did. Maybe he escapes press censure because he is a West Indian, and therefore, in spite of his colour, is not the bête noir of the Australian media. So, the question that arises is whether these incessant attacks on Jardine's personality were not merely an additional weapon in the complaint about the tactic. Jardine was a quiet, withdrawn sort of person, who, as Harold Larwood has described him, was like an actor on stage; he changed when he entered the cricket field.

The fact that Jardine kept an injured Larwood on the field, even when not bowling, whilst Bradman was still at the crease, is described by Mark Baldwin in his 2005 book *The Ashes' Strangest Moments* as an indication that Jardine was 'obsessed with using the very presence of Larwood to intimidate Bradman.' Obsessed? This was precisely the sort of tactic that Steve Waugh would have proudly proclaimed to be part of his Australian psychological warfare, his 'mental disintegration' strategy, but when it is Jardine, an intelligent tactic of subtle pressure becomes an 'obsession'. This incident has been mentioned by others as a measure of Jardine's ruthlessness. Asked about it 60 years later, Harold Larwood said that at the time he didn't twig to the reason behind it, but looking back, he understood the subtle psychological pressure being maintained on Bradman. "Mr Jardine," he said, "was quite nice about it – no sharp orders or anything like that. He just told me he wanted me to stay on the field, but it would have been better if he had quietly explained the reason behind his thinking to me at the time." Harold's account of Jardine's manner seems at odds with David Frith's later description of Jardine snapping, "You can't go off while this little bastard's in". In his own book, Harold says that those words were used, but he explained later Jardine said it quietly. However, Frith's version seems unlikely because if Jardine had really said it in a 'snapping' fashion, presumably the batsman at the other end would have heard him and that obviously would have revealed his game plan to Bradman. Bradman was to be encouraged to think that Larwood might be brought on to bowl again and therefore perhaps take chances in making as many runs as he could in the meantime. The strategy seems to have worked, for not long afterwards, he was dismissed by Verity for 71. The Australian innings soon collapsed after that.

Following the fourth Test at Brisbane, Jardine made the following statement:

For the last two months I have been receiving a regular host of letters of goodwill from Australians, and I would like to take this opportunity of thanking them and assuring them that their letters have been greatly appreciated by members of the team and myself.

The number of these letters alone has prevented me from answering them personally. It is, however, just these correspondents who appreciate silence instead of comment and criticism from visitors and guests in matters of controversy. They would, I think, echo the hope that the game of cricket is all that matters, and the best and only thing is to go on with it, for there is nothing wrong with it.

Personally, I have been thrice lucky in the side which it has been my proud privilege to lead, and no captain, I feel sure, has received, or could ask for, greater help, sympathy and utter loyalty than has fallen to my fortunate lot. We are proud of our fortune and success against our gallant and determined opponents, under Mr Woodfull, and condole with them on their sad loss through the death of Mr Archie Jackson.

It is likely that most people will never have heard of this statement, for it does not fit in with the conventional portrayal of Douglas Jardine. However, it was reported in the Australian press at the time, and has therefore always been there.

Even in the 21st century and some 50 years after his death, the long-still corpse of Douglas Jardine continues to be assiduously picked over by cricket-writing carrion hunters seeking any possible morsel for continued criticism of the man. Every one of those who have exaggerated or distorted reported events involving Douglas Jardine during his 1932/33 tour waited until he was long gone before they wrote as they did. After all, to do so while he was alive would have allowed him to respond or explain and that might have defeated the purpose. He could have done so but he would probably have ignored them.

Let us consider two further possibilities. Had Jardine been a jovial, gregarious, beer drinking extrovert, who nevertheless pursued leg-theory as a tactic, would the Australians have made their complaints about bodyline so readily? On the other hand, portray Jardine as an aloof, haughty, conde-scending, English upper-class snob and invent the fiction that he is disliked by the whole English team, and the complaints about his tactics have an increased impression of validity and are more easily justified. Not for one moment is any of this to say that Douglas Jardine was an easy man to know. He clearly was not, but that isn't a crime. There are many who are funda-mentally shy, but that doesn't mean they suffer from some dire psychological condition. There are lots of people who lack spontaneity and are not extrovert wits, but that doesn't prove aloofness or snobbery. Almost any one of us has at one time or another been impatient, but that does not necessarily indicate innate lack of courtesy. There are two sides to every coin and a balanced view is required here – balance that seems to have been sadly lacking. As Plum Warner said in *The Book of Cricket*, 'Jardine is a many-sided man.'

As to attitudes towards barracking, Neville Cardus recounts an occasion in 1921 when Australian captain Warwick Armstrong sat on the grass at Old Trafford and refused to go on with the game because, unusual for matches in England, the crowd was barracking him. Armstrong was getting a dose of his own country's medicine. Maybe others who have criticised Jardine for ignoring the Australian barrackers found some reason to rationalise Armstrong's behaviour, but let us consider this – just what would the critics have said if Douglas Jardine had sat on the grass at Adelaide, as Warwick Armstrong did at Old Trafford?

Douglas Jardine died of cancer in 1958. His ashes were scattered beside Loch Rannoch in his beloved Scottish Highlands.

Loch Rannoch: Jardine's last resting place.

WYATT AND ALLEN

"Nor do I think there is the smallest doubt that if Australia had had a bowler of the type of Larwood they would have bowled him in the same way we did. It was only common sense."

Bob Wyatt, 1951

"I have bowled fast at times out here and made the ball fly but never the leg-theory. I have refused to do it. Jardine said I ought to do it which made me furious."

Letter to his parents, Gubby Allen, 1932

THESE TWO MEMBERS of the team have mostly been portrayed as having been men of integrity who opposed Jardine's tactics. However research shows there to have been a totally different side in each case and Bob Wyatt's own published views are the opposite of the picture painted by others. Wyatt was Jardine's deputy on the 1932/33 tour and several authors, Le Quesne and Swanton for instance, have asserted that he was very much against the leg-theory tactic. However, Wyatt's own book *Three Straight Sticks* published some 18 years after that tour in 1951, states the very opposite:

The type of bowling employed by Larwood would certainly not have been so successful if used by any other fast bowler. Having so amazingly accurate a bowler as Larwood, I think Jardine was fully justified using him as he did. Certainly I don't want to shirk my share of the responsibility for the decision the Committee made.

These are not the views of a leg-theory opponent, but someone who simply sees the tactic as the logical way to employ a bowler of Larwood's unique ability. However, more tellingly Wyatt went even further, saying:

Nor do I think there is the slightest doubt that if Australia had had a bowler of the type of Larwood they would have used him in the same way we did. It was only commonsense.

It seems remarkable that these views, published by a man who was the vice-captain of the team, appear to have been ignored, perhaps because they detract from the theory that Jardine was the sole proponent of the leg-theory strategy. However Wyatt's comments seem fairly definite, as he is not talking about some emotional retaliation but simply of making the best use of the bowling attack at hand. When asked about what Wyatt had said in his book, Larwood's comment was, "I don't read cricket books. I don't need to as I have my own memories and knowledge so I don't know what was written but I can say Mr Jardine frequently consulted Mr Wyatt regarding field placing for leg-theory and the two of them seemed to be in agreement."

Le Quesne in his book *The Bodyline Controversy* states that Wyatt 'would never have countenanced bodyline', but it seems odd that he should have made this observation in 1983 some thirty years after Wyatt himself had gone to print to state precisely the opposite. The same is true of Swanton in his 1977 book *Follow On* wherein he states that Bob Wyatt was 'dead against bodyline'. As in the case of Le Quesne, Swanton's book came out only a few years after Wyatt's own book had indicated totally different views. In his book Wyatt also made the following observation:

The effect of Larwood lay not so much in the fact that he was bowling the occasional bouncer but in his almost miraculous control of length and direction. Bowling at that speed the bowler

Left, Bob Wyatt (vice-captain) and, right, Gubby Allen.
Both men wrote that they felt Jardine's strategy to be well-founded.
Wyatt went so far as to suggest he would have used Leg-theory had he been
captain and not Jardine.

has only to make a slight mistake in direction to present an easy target for the batsman. But Larwood was so accurate he gave very little away indeed.

Voce was also accurate and, although not as fast as Larwood, he bowled with his head. GO Allen never bowled better than on that tour, but he didn't bowl leg-theory, partly because he didn't approve of it and partly because he wasn't as fast as Larwood and would not be able to do it with such accuracy and pace.

Wyatt also points out that 19 of Larwood's 33 Test wickets were either bowled or LBW and therefore only a possible 14 could have fallen directly as a result of leg-theory. Voce took 15 wickets and of these 6 were either bowled or LBW leaving a balance of only 9 wickets possibly due to leg-theory. This produces a total between the two bowlers of 23 wickets that might have been due to leg-theory catches. According to Harold Larwood leg-theory was not used for the tail-enders and Swanton says this view is supported by Allen. Thirteen tail-end wickets were taken by either Larwood or Voce and therefore if these wickets are excluded the number of Australian wickets possibly lost to leg-theory falls to a total of 10. Given that a total of 93 Australian wickets fell to bowlers during the series, this figure of 10 means that only 11 per cent were due to leg-theory and this figure is a generous one because not all the 20 catches may have been taken when leg-theory was in operation. It might also be noted that at least 7 Australian wickets fell so early in an innings that leg-theory could not have been responsible.

A further issue that needs to be explored is the 'bodyline-would-not-have-occurred-without-Jardine' theory and again this brings in Bob Wyatt who says the first time on that tour that leg-theory was tried was under his captaincy at Melbourne, in a match against an Australian XI when Jardine was away on a fishing trip:

> It seemed so successful that the Selection Committee had a long discussion about it afterwards and from it they began to evolve the leg-theory plan, with the intention of defeating Bradman.

The Selection Committee consisted of Jardine, Wyatt, Sutcliffe, Hammond and Warner and the question that therefore arises is whether the same strategy would in fact have been pursued had Wyatt been captain and not Jardine? Wyatt's own comments would also seem to contradict Swanton's version that Wyatt and Allen reassured each other at the end of each day's play because of their shared loathing of Jardine's tactics. From Wyatt's own statements this seems unlikely. Asked about the friendship between Wyatt and Allen, Harold Larwood said it was not surprising. He pointed out that they were both amateurs, at a time when amateurs tended to stick together, and they were about the same age - in their early thirties. According to Larwood the other two amateurs, Brown and Pataudi were also frequently in each other's company, and again this seems to have been logical because they were ex-Oxford or Cambridge and about the same age – roughly ten years younger than Wyatt and Allen. Wyatt was yet another to say that the leg-theory strategy was made far more difficult for the Australian batsmen by the uneven bounce of their own wickets and Allen's biographer, Swanton, says that Allen made the same observation. The photograph on page 172 clearly shows an example of this. Woodfull is ducking a short ball he believes will rise but it actually strikes him on the back only a fraction above stump height; only a little lower and an LBW appeal might have been made.

Another member of the side who added fuel to the controversy was Allen, by publicly refusing to bowl leg-theory. Gubby Allen had been borne in Sydney but at 30 years of age was fairly old for a fast bowler making his first trip to Australia. He seems to have been something of a Warner protégée and certainly the two families were quite close. He had played sporadically for Middlesex over the previous 7/8 years with fluctuating success and his selection was generally regarded with some surprise. Allen was reasonably fast but at 30 this was hardly the age to be embarking on an arduous tour of a country where the climate can be very hot and the wickets hard and unhelpful. So there would seem to have been some inside influence in his selection and apparently he disagreed with leg-theory, in principle, or so he said. But as both Larwood and Wyatt have pointed out, he was neither fast nor accurate enough to have bowled it with any success, and he probably realised this himself. However, although claiming he was totally against the strategy, Allen was quite happy to field in Larwood's leg trap. In fact he took more catches (and some of them quite remarkable) off leg-theory at short leg than any other fielder in the England side and in Larwood's total Test career Allen took more catches off his bowling than either Chapman, Jardine, Ames or Hammond. Plum Warner, in his book *The Book of Cricket* specifically states, 'G O Allen made a great name for himself at short leg'. It seems odd that a man of such high principles disdained from bowling leg-theory but was quite prepared to act as co-executioner for someone else who was bowling it. If Allen was so against leg-theory then why didn't he insist on fielding at third-man, for instance, or cover point? Such positions were quite open to him and would not have compromised his sensitivities on the issue. Moreover, although he might not have conceded this, Allen probably benefited from bowling in tandem with Larwood on a number of occasions for many a wicket has fallen through a batsman unconsciously relaxing or taking risks when at the less hostile end.

Brian Rendell's 2003 book *Gubby Allen – Bad Boy of Bodyline?* was written following a detailed study of Allen's complete letters to his parents whilst on that tour and these are now kept in the Mitchell Library in Sydney. Rendell says he came to the clear conclusion that Allen's real motives had little to do with any moral misgivings regarding principle but were more concerned with his public image in Australia, the reaction of his relatives there, the worry that he might be damaging the reputation of his family and, moreover, that he did not believe he could bowl leg-theory as well as Larwood and Voce. This latter interpretation is perhaps reinforced by the discovery that in one of his letters Allen had referred to Larwood and Voce as 'swollen headed gutless uneducated miners' and if that was what he thought then he wouldn't have wanted to provide an unfavourable comparison. When discussing Allen with Harold Larwood in the early 1990s he made the point that more than anyone else in the side Allen always seem concerned about his image. Harold said he couldn't actually put a finger on it, but it was just an impression he gained. When he made that observation he couldn't have known what Allen's letters were to reveal, but his comment does now fall into an interesting perspective.

In another letter Allen wrote: 'Don Bradman made some incredible shots but he is a terrible little coward of fast bowling.' Fear when facing extreme pace is really an uneasy apprehension, and perfectly reasonable, but 'coward'? Rendell says he was informed by the Mitchell Library that the letter regarding Bradman had been 'restricted' until after Bradman's death since it was thought better to keep a lid on these views whilst he was still alive. Bradman had considered Allen to be a close friend and it would have come as something of a shock to discover what his friend had been writing about him. He wrote of the rest of the team as 'a collection of half-wits' in one letter and described Jardine as 'an absolute swine' in another. He would no doubt have been embarrassed had he known that early in 1933 Jardine was to write to his father, Sir Walter Allen, as follows:

Don Bradman: Gubby Allen dubbed him 'a terrible little coward of fast bowling' in a letter to his parents sent home from the tour.

Dear Sir Walter

Please excuse great haste and this paper – I have taken refuge here from Press man and Publishers who made my home pretty trying for my people to live in!

This is just another on Obbie – I don't think I am betraying any confidence if I give you my report to MCC as far as he is concerned, you know I will not broadcast it.

GO Allen set a truly magnificent example to the side, knocking off smoking and drinking – an excellent tourer in every way, and one who deserved every atom of success which came his way, and was, in fact unlucky - or so it seemed to me, in not having more success with the bat - a wonderful short leg.

I can't say more than that for I mean every word of it - how pleased and justly proud you and Lady Allen must be to have him back. I hope you are both very well. Your family were extraordinarily good to me in Australia.

In haste, yours sincerely,

Douglas R Jardine.

This letter seems to reveal a generous side to Jardine's character - after all Allen had been the source of some embarrassing public disputes regarding leg-theory and yet Jardine does not appear to have resented this at all.

In his book *Gubby Allen - Man of Cricket* Swanton says that at one point in the tour Allen had threatened Warner that he would report directly to Findlay, the MCC Secretary, if he was again asked to bowl leg-theory. Whether this was the 1930s public school hierarchy - an Old Etonian not taking orders from a mere Wykehamist - is not clear but it does indicate a somewhat difficult position for Jardine in that a member of the side of which he was the appointed captain was threatening to go over his head simply because he disliked a tactical point. This has an unhealthy quasi-political tinge to it, in that Allen knew or had been told he could ignore his captain and complain directly to Lord's. Allen wasn't even vice-captain but he seems to have been told by someone - Warner? - that he could act quite independently if he so wished, or maybe Warner was quietly encouraging him in this. One might have expected the response from a touring side manager to be that it would be improper to take any such action.

When away from cricket on that tour Allen was very much on a social whirl involving dinner parties, dances, golf, horse-racing, theatres and so on, and one of his reasons for declining to bowl leg-theory may have been to preserve his popularity in a country where sport was so intertwined at all levels of society. Although sometimes vitriolic in his criticism of Jardine he was nonetheless apparently quite happy to accept invitations to spend rest days in Jardine's company and happily mixed with him on a social basis.

Gubby Allen seems to emerge with some ambivalence, with some of his actions and statements strangely ambiguous. He went out of his way to emphasise widely his opposition to the very principle of leg-theory and yet happily functioned as one of the most effective assistants. He privately and publicly criticised Douglas Jardine and yet was quite happy to keep company with him socially. All in all, Allen seems to have been a strange collection of contradictions.

Other than Jardine himself, Wyatt and Allen were the two leading amateurs in a side that contained five non-professionals. It is therefore worth considering the overall position of the amateur in English cricket in the early 1930s.

ENGLAND AND AMATEUR CONTROL

"I trust no professional will ever captain England."

Lord Hawke, 1925

"I was earning a good living out in the fresh air, with green grass under my feet; why would I risk that by openly questioning anything, however flawed it might be?"

Harold Larwood, 1992

AT THE TIME of the 1932/33 series, cricket in England was played within a totally different social context when compared with today. This may well be because it is true of society in general that much has altered in the almost seven decades since the tour. In 1932 England was a country where there were distinct class divisions, where the aristocracy still held sway and where the British public school was regarded as the nursery from which there emerged, as of right, the country's future leaders. Douglas Jardine's schooling and cricket were typical of this milieu.

Although by and large it produced people, for the most part men, who could be relied upon to behave with decorum and honesty, the system seemed to have cared little about whether these leaders were effective or efficient. The attitude towards life and the world as a whole appears to have been that it was far better to lose, anything apparently, the right way rather than achieve success in a manner that might carry with it any question of probity. This philosophy was a major influence in English cricket and affected England's performances at Test level.

Times have changed. No longer does the 'gentleman' hold sway on the cricket fields of England. But at the time of the 1932/33 Australian tour the amateur was very much in control. Indeed during the period between World Wars I and II, an average of something like 25 per cent of all players appearing in County cricket were amateurs. However every County captain was an amateur. It was even thought desirable that every England team should contain a certain quota of amateurs. This was a reflection of the social mores of that era, which appear to have dictated that the priority in selecting the England team was to maintain the position of the amateur rather than to pick the best possible eleven. The effect on England's prospects and the selection of less than the best available team was therefore justified in the interests of maintaining the social order, although it was not necessarily seen that way in all quarters. It may be said that had England's teams been selected on merit, as they were in Australia, England would have been more successful than they were. It is not clear whether those in positions of authority within the game in England genuinely believed in some Corinthian ideal whereby only they and their class could provide the necessary influence, or whether they felt that by allowing ability and performance to be the sole considerations for selection, many would have been signing their own death warrants. It may have been that the claims of moral guidance, the priorities of class, culture, courtesy and convention were felt to be of genuine importance by those in authority and thus justified the continuation of their own existence. Another possibility is that this influence was genuinely believed to be necessary to prevent County cricket in England from becoming the sort of fierce competition that was to characterise cricket in Australia. There, although the technical standard could not be criticised, the atmosphere of abrasive confrontation would have spoiled the ethos of the English County game.

Sir Pelham Warner was a figure of some prominence and influence in the history of cricket. In his biography *Plum Warner* Gerald Howat recounts that critics identified Warner with:

a conservatism in attitude and convention in which cricket had a secure niche within a structured and sheltered social order. Cricket, he believed, was one of the lynchpins that strengthened the foundations of that society.

This description probably encapsulates the naïve and innocent beliefs of those whose social backgrounds gave them charge of the game in England.

In the early 1930s, England was largely run by an establishment whose approach to a wide range of issues seems to have avoided the realities of competition and commercialism, and so within this context, cricket was no different. To be competitive, in any sphere, required ability, experience, initiative and intelligence, whereas in many areas the ruling strata could produce merely a style of education. To give priority to considerations of efficiency and performance on a widespread basis would have threatened the existing order. But it was a blinkered honourable world of monocles and whiskers, almost childlike in its naïve beliefs, a world that would disappear with World War II with the need to come out victorious in that conflict. To a large extent this philosophy represented the educational priorities of the times. The purpose of a university was to produce cultivated human beings rather than engineers or physicians with the Humanities, and above all the Classics, as the prestige degrees. Technology, engineering and trade as a whole were regarded as vulgar. This meant that cricket was regarded as some fine artistic calling, and thus only the gentleman could provide the right sort of leadership. The Classics man would have looked upon the professionals as he looked upon trade - essential but only to be involved in when absolutely necessary. It has been said by Corelli Barnett in *Audit of War* that this line of thinking was largely responsible for Britain's relative decline as a major industrial power. The GNP of the United States overtook that of the UK in 1904 but hardly anyone noticed or was concerned. After all, the British Empire was at its zenith. Possibly contributing to this industrial decline was the fact that in 1913 the UK had just three technical colleges, whereas in Germany there were over thirty. This perception of trade as unimportant carried over into cricket and this perhaps contributed to the priority given by 'gentlemen' to 'playing the game' and 'form' rather than the result. Jack Hobbs wrote that in England 'the result does not matter so much as the play', and he compared this attitude with the Australian view that the result was the only consideration. Cricket in England was viewed almost as an art form, to be enjoyed as such and if it became too competitive, this might result in the exclusion of those who played County cricket for their own enjoyment and not for a living.

Writing in the mid-1930s, George Orwell stated that cricket 'gives expression to a well-marked trait in the English character, the tendency to value "form" or "style" more highly than success'. This philosophy still has its adherents in the 21st century. The September 2003 Newsletter of the Hampshire Cricket Society complained that it was unfair to blame the County Championship when England did badly at international level, saying that it was purely the performance of the selected individuals who were responsible. Just how Test performances were separated from the competition where the craft had been learned was not explained. Similarly in the Spring 2005 edition of the Journal of the Cricket Society, there appeared an article questioning why most of the modern media believed the County Championship existed solely to produce a winning England Test team. Both articles seemingly viewed the County Championship as some detached art form with no practical role to play. Both of them displayed an unrealistic and nostalgic yearning for a game that could be played as if the rest of the world did not exist. Herein lies much of the differences between English and Australian attitudes. It may be claimed that it is not the sole purpose of the County Championship to produce successful international sides, but if that is not its main aim and it is just a jolly domestic competition, then where do the England selectors look for players of sufficient quality with which to compose their Test XIs? The County Championship gradually evolved and was never envisaged at the outset as the basis and nursery for cricketers to play at international level. This has come about almost by accident, simply because there is no other source and because within this evolving structure each County continued to retain considerable autonomy.

In Australia by comparison, cricket was organised competitively from an early stage on "grade" levels, culminating in a team for each State and thence a Test side. It is a pyramid selection process carefully designed to nurture and produce players of international ability and it has been very successful. Until fairly recently, State cricket was not professional, but playing a Grade match over two weekends meant that a level of hard competitiveness could be maintained with a five day breather in between, a level which would not be possible playing on the day-to-day basis of the County Championship. After his first season playing County Cricket, Australian Test batsman Dean Jones said that because of the day-to-day nature of the County Championship it would be an impossibility to maintain the same level of fierce competition that characterised Grade cricket in Australia. Thus, the priorities of form and style hampered the selection and performances of English cricket teams, whereas the Australians, by contrast, looked solely for and at results. This has been a significant contributory factor in explaining why Australia has generally held the upper hand. In this respect it is interesting to note the recent 'spirit of cricket' ladder in the County Championship, introduced at the behest of MCC. There are no points involved and the ratings count for nothing in terms of success at the end of the season but the published list does provide an indication of which Counties played more according to the intended spirit of the game rather than merely for results and success rates. Clearly the intention of the MCC is that success during the season should not be calculated solely in figures. In Australia by comparison there is no similar State rating, which seems once more to highlight the difference in priorities between the two countries. This English attitude would assist in explaining the success in County cricket between the two World Wars of a bowler like leg-spinner Titch Freeman. It was considered bad form, particularly for an amateur, not to have a go at him, resulting in many stumpings or catches in the outfield and a career total of 3,776 wickets at an average of 18. The Australians, understandably, would have none of this silly philosophy and played each ball on its merits. As a result and by comparison with his career figures, Freeman's Test record against Australia showed a meagre return of 8 wickets at an average of 57.

In 1926 the *Daily Express* stated that a professional captain would be necessary if England were to win the Ashes. The paper did not elaborate but what this meant was that the eleven selected should represent the best available rather than the position of captain being reserved for an amateur. This argument would have been regarded by English cricket hierarchy as bolshevism and so the article was not widely published. A privileged place was reserved in society as a whole at that time for those with money and/or those who had been educated at a public school. However had every England side been selected solely on merit and performance, as were the Australians, there would frequently have been no place for an amateur. The situation might then have arisen wherein the national side consisted only of professionals and the only place for the amateurs was at County level. Obviously this could not be allowed to occur because it would have exposed the privileged position of the amateur as little more than social decoration and therefore under whatever rationale was available the status quo was continued. Pelham Warner even went so far in 1921 as to claim that it was "public school spirit which made us come out on top in the Great War". No doubt Warner sincerely believed this, although the many thousands who lost their lives on the first day of the battle of the Somme might have had some reservations about that notion.

County and England sides were run rather like country estates, with the professionals being the gamekeepers, grooms and gardeners. The effective functioning of these technicians would have been thought impossible without the leadership of 'the Squire'. Many County sides consisted of ten cricketers and one 'nice chap', who was captain of course, although it must be said that some of the 'nice chaps' were indeed accomplished cricketers. Australians no doubt viewed this quaint and obsolete social apartheid with amusement or even outright derision. A number of County captains could not have held their places on merit alone and there were several England captains whose performances make it clear that they were little more than passengers, included in the national side by the selectors' social priorities. For the 1927/28 tour of South Africa, due initially to the illness of the first captain selected, Guy Jackson of Derbyshire, and presumably because there was no one else who could be considered, the selectors raked up Lt Col R.T. Stanyforth as captain of the side. Stanyforth had played no Test cricket at all and only three County games and was then aged 35. During that tour he appeared in 4 Tests and managed a total of 13 runs at an average of 2.60. In fairness it should be added that as a wicket-keeper he caught 7 and stumped 2. Even 20 years later and after the class levelling necessary for victory in World War II, the selectors apparently could still not bring themselves to countenance the prospect of a professional captain. For the 1947/48 tour of the West Indies, Gubby Allen was brought out of retirement. He was then 45, his Test career had rested on his fast bowling and he hadn't played Test cricket for ten years. During that series Allen played in three Tests, scoring 94 runs at an average of 18.8 and took just 5 wickets for 205 runs. For the remaining Test, Cranston, an amateur, was stand-in captain.

An added advantage held by the amateurs is that they seem to have been able to move from one County to another without question. Bob Wyatt, for instance, moved from Warwickshire to Worcestershire; Freddie Brown, Surrey to Northants; CB Fry, Sussex to Hampshire; Raman Subba Row, Surrey to Northants; Desmond Eagar, Gloucester to Hampshire, etc. This freedom was not available to the professionals. For the most part, they accepted their lot rather than jeopardise their position, even if they privately resented the system. Harold Larwood was a fairly mild personality, but as he put it to the author:

> Here I was being paid at least as much as I would have earned in the dirt and dark of a coal mine, but moreover earning a good and enjoyable living out in the fresh air, with green grass under my feet; why would I risk that by openly questioning anything, however flawed it might be?

A large proportion of professional County cricketers, particularly in the midlands and north of England, had got themselves out of the sweat, grime and filth of the pits, mills and factories for a much better and healthier lifestyle. So although the professionals did often discuss their situation amongst themselves vis-à-vis the privileged position of the amateurs, as Harold recalled, the general consensus was not to make waves because it would not have achieved anything. This al fresco lifestyle did not last all year, but it was a big improvement and many of those who made a name for themselves were offered alternative employment opportunities outside the cricket season. Even for those who worked 'in the sun', it was still an opportunity. Some professionals returned to the land outside the cricket season but just prior to World War I, when a farm labourer's weekly wage was nine shillings, George Bernard Shaw was complaining that he couldn't get a decent meal in London for less than three shillings and sixpence.

So marked was the difference between amateur and professional that in many County grounds the amateurs had their own dressing room and the professionals another. In some grounds, they even walked onto the field of play through different gates. It was as if there was something contagious about the professionals from which the amateurs had to be protected. It is not difficult to imagine the reaction and response of egalitarian Australians to this almost feudal structure. In many Counties the July/August period saw the arrival of university players and schoolmasters, cricketers who 'played for fun'. It was assumed that for the most part the professionals didn't mind this, provided these amateurs were good enough and, apart from saving money, in many Counties increasing the amateur content was thought to be a good thing. The professionals however were never consulted, nor were they asked if the loss of their match fees would mean any financial hardship. There were those who did openly question the clear prejudice in favour of cricketers who had little other than money to justify their position, but they usually paid the price. Charlie Parker the Gloucester left-arm spinner, who was well known for his attitude towards the system, had an altercation with Plum Warner and it has been said that this was the reason he was not picked for England. In fact the confrontation was the result of his frustration at non-selection and not the cause of it, for this occurred in April 1929 when Parker was already 46 years of age. Parker was a contemporary of Wilfred Rhodes, but he was a different type of bowler, both being left-arm spinners, but Parker was quicker than Rhodes and turned the ball more. Although taking 3,278 wickets at an average of 19.46 in a career from 1903 to 1935, he played in only one Test match, against Australia in 1921, with very respectable figures of 2 for 32 in 28 overs. At the time of his argument with Warner he had taken over 1600 wickets at an average of around 17 since the end of World War I. Had England teams during the 1920s and 1930s been picked on merit and what was needed to maximise England's prospects, then Parker would probably have been a regular choice and if he had bowled in tandem with Rhodes, they would have formed a deadly duo unmatched anywhere in the world at that time, but he had questioned the selectors' priorities and in so doing had removed himself from consideration. Another case was that of professional Joe Hardstaff jnr. Hardstaff had been commissioned during World War II and, having rubbed shoulders with other officers, he emerged from his army duties with an attitude towards amateurs that was different from that of 1939. This slightly more casual approach irritated Gubby Allen on the 1947/48 tour of the West Indies who regarded this familiarity as bordering on insubordination and as a result Hardstaff played in only one more Test. Moreover, this occurred at a time when England was desperate for middle-order batsmen. Hardstaff played in 23 Test matches, making over 1,600 runs at an average of 46.74. Like Warner, Allen the amateur was something of an authoritarian figure and felt that the professionals should know their place.

But this divide was not only a question of attitude towards the establishment. In 1951 Cambridge Blue and England batsman/wicket-keeper, Paul Gibb, joined Essex as a professional. That a Varsity Blue was found playing cricket for a wage apparently appalled MCC to such an extent that a special committee was established to investigate and resulted in Gibb's MCC membership being withdrawn. The MCC worthies responsible for this decision must have turned in their graves when a very worthy gentleman, ex-professional Tom Graveney, became MCC President in 2005. In 1960, Jim Laker, possibly the greatest Test off-spinner ever, published his book *Over To Me*, which today reads as totally innocuous. But at that time the powers that be regarded some of the comments in the book as too critical of the establishment and so, irrespective of Laker's standing, his MCC membership was withdrawn. It should be added that this strange error of judgement was later rescinded.

But even years later, such snobbery could emerge from time to time. During a County match in the 1970s between Hampshire and Leicestershire at Southampton, Ray Illingworth, the Leicestershire captain, was introduced in the pavilion to George Taylor who had captained Hampshire in 1939. Illingworth shook Taylor by the hand and said, "Nice to meet you, George." An innocent enough rejoinder it might be thought. However, Taylor limped away from this encounter, wringing his hand and complaining, "Bloody man called me George!" Taylor, who didn't bowl, had played 24 times for

Hampshire, making a total of 306 runs at an average of 9.27. Worcester and England leg spinner Roly Jenkins was yet another case where a flippant attitude towards the amateur was cause for his Test selections to be prejudiced. There is the famed episode that took place after he had produced a well-written piece on spin-bowling. Walter Robins, who apparently did not believe that a mere professional could have been so erudite, asked him who had written it for him. Jenkins replied, "I wrote it myself, Sir. Who read it for you?" However, the final nail went into the coffin of his Test prospects when he made the tongue-in-cheek comment to some character in a multi-coloured cap that he thought he might play as an amateur that day since he wanted to catch the early train back to Worcester. Today such remarks would be considered totally harmless and clever wit but, at that time, this lack of deference found its way back to Lords. Roly Jenkins was carpeted and never again played for England and this happened despite the fact that his Test bowling average rivalled that of other leg-spinners such as Doug Wright or Eric Hollies. His number of wickets per Test was better than theirs and he was a far better bat than either of them.

Harold Larwood said that Jardine's attitude towards the professionals was different to that of Warner and Allen. Although Jardine was very much the skipper, Harold said he always called them by their first names, whereas although Warner was friendly enough, it was surnames only. Harold said this was also true of Allen, who always referred to the professionals by their surnames. The other two young amateurs, Brown and Pataudi, were treated very much as equals and responded as such. Warner's attitude was still there as late as 1951 when he was President of the MCC. At a joint MCC and National Book League exhibition, he went out of his way to say that he deplored the use of a cricketer's Christian name by writers like John Arlott, declaring that he felt it "reduced their dignity". The underlying snobbery in this statement was clear, and Arlott angrily retorted that he preferred to refer to Denis Compton as if he were his friend, not his groom. In reality, of course, Warner was not concerned about dignity at all, but rather the risk of friendly familiarity leading to equality that would threaten the established distinction of the amateur. Although Warner had given much service to cricket he had been born in 1873 and had difficulty in shaking off the class attitudes with which he had been imbued as a boy in the West Indies.

This social apartheid continued at club cricket levels where it was refined still further. Cricket author Stephen Chalke recounts the case of Kent's John Pretlove, who although he had been to a public school and had been a Cambridge Blue, in 1955 was refused entry to the Band of Brothers cricket club because his father was in 'trade'.

The extent to which England's performances were hamstrung by the liability of the amateur priority is demonstrated by a comparison of the batting averages of five opposing England and Australian captains during the 1920-1950 period. Ignoring Gilligan, who was solely a bowler, the combined Test batting average of Chapman, Allen, Wyatt, Yardley and Brown is 27. On the Australian side, the combined average of Armstrong, Collins, Ryder, Woodfull and Hassett is 46, and that is without Bradman, who was in a league of his own. These figures are for all Test matches and are not confined to the Ashes contests. Jardine was head and shoulders above the rest of the English amateur captains of that time, with a Test batting average of 48. If one accepts, as a rule of thumb, that any Test batsman who averages over 45 is of the highest class, this puts Jardine into some fairly rarefied company. Taking as a qualification a minimum of 20 innings, only eleven English batsmen have a higher Test batting average than 48 - Sutcliffe, Paynter, Barrington, Hammond, Hobbs, Hutton, Tyldesley, Pietersen, Compton, Mead and Jackson. To be fair this list with 20 innings as a qualification would exclude K.S. Duleepsinhji, who in 19 innings averaged 58.52, but even then there are only twelve ahead of Jardine.

The difference in the respective captains' contributions is considerable and only goes to demonstrate the degree to which Australia was advantaged by their policy of always picking their best XI and then appointing a captain from those selected if an existing captain were not in place. It might be said that in many instances an Australian 11 was playing against an England 10.5. Whilst it was not quite a case of Colonel Blimp versus Erwin Rommel, the price England paid for this policy of amateur priority is fairly clear. This is not to say that none of England's amateurs deserved their place on ability and performance alone. Post World War II, for instance, England was blessed with outstanding amateur batsmen such as May, Cowdrey and Dexter, all of whom were England captains, but in general terms it was not a policy that produced the best side available.

There is an additional dimension to the differing approaches regarding contributions to the national team. Shane Warne played far more games for Australia than he did for his home State of Victoria, but there was not a squeak of complaint about him not being available for Victoria. Compare this with the complaints from various Counties and their Members when their players are told to rest rather than get involved in a County match between Tests. Australia concentrates and guards its Test resources. In England there are quite a number who want to have their cake and eat it too.

The picture of priorities that emerges is one wherein the social order had to be maintained at all cost and was of far greater importance than the level of playing skill available to England. It had to be made clear that no challenge to the existing order would be tolerated. The Australians were comfortably accustomed to the advantage this gave them – until 1932/33, and then along came Douglas Jardine who was just as hard as they had always been, and a very good bat as well.

TEST CAPTAINS

"'Australianism' means single-minded determination to win –
to win within the laws but, if necessary, to the last limit
within them."

John Arlott, 1949

"I was prepared to be as ruthless as it takes to stuff you. I didn't
mind upsetting anyone, my own team-mates included, as long as
I got the right result."

Alan Border, 1989

IT IS IMPORTANT to understand how England's cricket performances had, undoubtedly, been hampered by a social priority for some considerable time. Despite this, it appears to have been accepted in England that the amateur quota would be pursued, apparently irrespective of consequences. The Australians were accustomed to this eccentricity in their English opponents and would probably have recognised that it gave them an advantage.

In Douglas Jardine, however, they were to encounter a man whose social background and education were impeccably establishment, but whose approach was some way ahead of his time and was just as hard and unyielding as their own. Within this class scenario there were nonetheless amateur cricketers who could justify a place in the 1932/33 touring team on performances alone. Jardine himself was described by author Ronald Mason as 'at times not only a very good player but a great player.' Jardine played no cricket in 1929 and very little in 1930, but, in the five County seasons from 1927 to 1932, he had accumulated 5,105 runs at an average of 63.81. In 1927 and 1928 he was top of the batting averages; in 1931 he was third, and in 1932, in eighth position. In 11 Test matches over 4 years against Australia, India, New Zealand and the West Indies, he had made 683 runs at an average of 56.9. He was worth his place in the side for his batting alone.

Bob Wyatt, nominated as vice-captain, had played and toured for England for several years with reasonable success, had captained one Test against Australia in 1930 and had been well up in the batting averages for some seasons. In addition, there was the *sine qua non* that he was an amateur, thus his selection would have made sense. An amateur who would have been an automatic choice was the brilliant K.S. Duleepsinhji but he had been dogged by tubercular ill health for some time and was forced to withdraw. His place probably went to the Nawab of Pataudi. In 1931 whilst at Oxford, Pataudi had been second in the County Championship batting averages with 1454 at an average of 69, and in 1932, playing for Worcester, he averaged 46.62 and he was still only 22 years old. Although dropped after the first two Tests because of his vulnerability to the spin of O'Reilly and Ironmonger, Pataudi scored well in all other matches, making five centuries. However, later experience for both England and then India showed that he was not quite up to Test standard.

The remaining amateurs in the party were Allen and Brown. Brown was only 21 when selected and had given glimpses of possibilities at international level. He had been selected for two of the Tests against New Zealand in 1931, he'd had a good season as an all-rounder in 1932 and had played in the one Test against India that year, but in none of the Tests did he show any real potential. His selection, therefore, may have been due to a need to fill the amateur 'quota'. In addition to his batting, he could bowl both medium-pace and leg-breaks and so was possibly thought worth a slot in the party as an all-rounder. Brown's performance, however, was something of a disappointment. Although he played in only the State and minor matches and took 24 wickets, his batting did not come up to expectations. Allen is considered in a separate chapter but his selection does seem to have been something of a mystery.

What does all this have to do with Jardine and the 1932/33 tour? Simply that although the social and cricket setting of the time was as described, in Douglas Jardine the England selectors had picked an amateur whose cricketing ability alone clearly justified his selection in the team. Moreover, they had appointed as captain a man with a very professional approach to the game. He was an amateur, in that he did not earn his living by being directly paid for playing cricket, but it might be said that he was England's first professional captain in his analysis, strategy and execution. Whether his appointment was as unwitting as has been suggested is open to question; it seems more likely that it was deliberate, but when the balloon went up everyone ran for cover. Given the need to find an answer to the Bradman run-making machine the decision was probably made to have a captain who would be as single-minded and determined as necessary, as Bradman was himself and to appoint a lesser soul would be futile. After the event, when all the dust caused by what almost exploded into a diplomatic incident had settled, those involved appeared to distance themselves from the matter, and Jardine and Larwood were left to carry the can.

Up until Jardine's appointment, the Australians had been accustomed to a series of 'nice jovial chaps' as English captains, all of whom would have died rather than be thought discourteous or cunning in their manner of play. Suddenly Australia was confronted with a totally different style of English leadership, one that was very professional and as clinical, shrewd and relentless as theirs had always been. Australian captains have mostly been fairly ruthless in their pursuit of victory, which is not to say that the rules were not, basically, observed. Rarely has Australia produced an engaging personality as leader, although there have been exceptions such as Lindsay Hassett, Richie Benaud and Mark Taylor. These were outside the stony-faced mould, but mostly the captains have been of the ilk of the abrasive Armstrong, clinical Bradman, the rugged Chappells, sledging Border and the merciless Steve Waugh – men for whom Test cricket was grim warfare and to be approached as such. Leaders who were virtual Obergruppenfuhrers in their cold, implacable and relentless pursuit of victory. In order to imbue them with the necessary fighting inspiration for the coming 2001 Ashes 'war' in England, Australian captain Steve Waugh led his team to Gallipoli, the scene of Australia's ANZAC sacrifices during the Dardanelles fighting of World War I. The Gallipoli campaign is commemorated with considerable reverence each year in Australia but Waugh's psychological tactic was rather like an England football team visiting the D-Day beaches before playing Germany.

As has been mentioned earlier, Walter Hammond had described Jardine as a captain who was imperturbable, calm, coldly determined to win, etc, and said that Australians did not like such an attitude. He also observed that those very characteristics would have described more than one Australian captain of his era. In fact, with the benefit of hindsight, it can be seen that Hammond's description of Jardine's approach could describe most Australian captains since that time and what seems to have contributed to the emerging atmosphere was that Jardine appeared in Australia with a markedly different approach from the previous visiting England captains.

It is not clear under which Australian captain 'sledging' first made its appearance in the Test arena, but it was around the era of Ian Chappell. The *Australian Concise Oxford Dictionary* notes that sledging originated in Australian cricket, and states the meaning as 'to taunt an opposing batsman to undermine his confidence'. Ian Chappell was an aggressive and abrasive character, so it may have been he who started it and the Australian press openly endorsed sledging as part of the aggressive tradition of Australian sport. Banter had always been a part of cricket and it is said that the level of good-humoured repartee when Keith Miller was batting, with Godfrey Evans keeping and Denis Compton at slip, was worthy of the best comedy show, but it was only flippant humour. Dry wit has always been part of cricket and as long as it is just that – humour – it adds to the spirit of the game. In 1930 when playing Yorkshire, one of the Essex opening batsmen played a ball firmly onto his middle stump. The bails flew into the air and then fell back into the grooves at the top of the three stumps. There was a moment's total silence and then came the voice of Emmott Robinson from second slip: "Ah say, has't thee tried walking on't water?"

It was during the 1970s in Australia that this banter descended to offensive personal jibes. Comments about what the batsmen's wife was up to whilst he was away, his social or racial ancestry and anything in order to put him off or interrupt his concentration, remarks usually coming from behind his back as he was just about to receive a ball. In this context it seems likely that one of the reasons Tony Greig was made England captain in 1974 was as a counter to the aggressive sledging of Ian Chappell. Greig was not exactly abrasive but he took no stick from anyone. However given the style of rhetoric regularly employed in politics in Australia, it is perhaps not surprising that their cricketers should have followed the example of their political leaders. One politician, a Prime Minister, Paul Keating, described the Opposition as "a collection of scumbags" and the Senate as "un-elected swill" and a State Treasurer has recently described a piece of Federal legislation as "shithouse". With this sort of example from those in the public eye, it is likely the advent of offensive and taunting sledging as a cricket tactic in Australia should come as no surprise. Australian politicians regularly hurl personal abuse at one another in Parliament, using language in a violent confrontational approach that would cause them to be permanently banned from Westminster. Consequently, it may have been a natural progression that a similar style of attack on the person should filter down to Australian cricket and also influence cricket barracking. As John Arlott once put it, "cricket more than any other sport reflects the times and the society in which it is played". Indeed, the behaviour, tactics and language in the New South Wales Parliament are frequently of such a questionable level that schools now hesitate to organise student trips to view parliamentary proceedings because of the examples to which children will be exposed. It would seem there is good reason why the New South Wales Parliament is known throughout Australia as 'the bear pit'.

Even in Australia itself, Allan Border was known as 'captain grumpy'. He had appeared fairly affable during the 1985 tour of England, but had lost the Test series. His cultivation of friendly relations with his opposite number, David Gower, was severely criticised in certain quarters in Australia (believed to be Ian Chappell) and, when he next visited England as captain for the 1989 tour, his attitude had completely changed. He refused to speak to Gower unless he absolutely had to and was the chief sledger, continuously taunting Gower with sneers such as "pretty boy Pom" and even worse. He had decided to be as unpleasant as was necessary to win and Australia did win that series and so from that point of view the end had justified the means. But what was the cause for this confrontation and abuse? It seems that Border was hell-bent on that most worthless of causes - revenge. Revenge for what it may be asked? Quite simply retribution for having inflicted what was seen and felt as humiliation for having lost the two previous Test series. England had not been seeking to inflict humiliation, merely to win, but this aspect of the Australian psyche has been mentioned earlier and it is a measure of the depth of feeling that Border was prepared to go to almost any lengths to avoid another loss. This win at all costs attitude of Border was implemented some fifty years after the 1932/33 tour and it may be asked where is the connection? Quite simply that this is the country that complained so very bitterly about Jardine's attitude and tactics and with this history one might have thought they would have been careful not to fall into the same mould. Not so. When the opportunity arose Australia has been quite happy to use any strategy that could help it win.

In 2006, Steve Waugh told the BBC he felt one of the reasons England had won back the Ashes in 2005 was that Australian relations with England had been too "friendly". "They were using England players' nicknames in the press and that was something that hadn't been done before", he said. What was clearly being demanded was a return to the open 'waughfare' that had characterised his reign over the troops. In the same year similar comments were made in the Australian press by Allan Border and Merv Hughes both saying that Australia had been far too friendly with England in the 2005 Ashes series and this had been a main factor in Australia's loss. That such an aggressive no holds barred mentality should be so widely encouraged and apparently publicly supported would seem to make any complaint from the Australian camp regarding spirit somewhat difficult to justify. Interestingly, the British press does not appear to have noticed this or, if they did, perhaps they felt it was par for the course. Even the British tabloids appear to have been very lenient on Border and Waugh. By contrast, what might the reaction of the Australian press have been if such a tactic had first been introduced by an English captain? Steve Waugh publicly proclaimed sledging to be part of his attempt to achieve what he described as "mental disintegration". No less a person than Sir Donald Bradman said he would never have allowed it, and yet the Australian cricket authorities did nothing about it.

It has been said that Jardine never forgot being denied a century in the Oxford match against Australia in 1921 when he was 98 not out when the Australians decided time was up. It has further been alleged that he regarded it as a slight from a 'colonial'. Although it makes good press there is no record anywhere of any resentment on the part of Jardine, neither of his ever having mentioned the incident, however, the story helps those seeking to justify their theory that Jardine hated Australians. It should be noted that due to a primitive scoreboard, the Australians may not even have been aware of Jardine's score, but it was another of the Australian hard men – Warwick Armstrong – who made the decision to call off play. This episode does compare interestingly with the generous treatment that Bradman received from Hampshire in 1930. It was his first tour to England and he needed 46 to make 1,000 runs in the month of May when the Australians came to Southampton on May 31. Hampshire, captained by Lord Tennyson, was dismissed for 151 and, in Australia's innings, Bradman made 39 when it started to rain and rain heavily. Despite the downpour, Tennyson kept Hampshire on the field, and Jack Newman bowled two easy full tosses that Bradman duly dispatched to the boundary to achieve his 1000 runs. Only then was play called off for the day. This decision was later excused by Tennyson who said that the full tosses might be explained by a slippery ball but given Newman's long and accomplished experience, this seems highly unlikely. It was undoubtedly a gesture of generosity in keeping with a certain spirit of cricket, but to put that into context, would Armstrong have offered anything similar? Jardine himself played very little cricket in 1930, but he may have noted the incident.

With this spectrum of Test captains for comparison, just what was the basis for the Australian complaint about Jardine, even without the factor of leg-theory? Was it not, as Walter Hammond has said, that even before he arrived, the press in Australia had decided they didn't like him and so almost whatever he did was going to be scrutinised, dissected, put under a microscope, with some factor distorted or invented for complaint or criticism?

This chapter quotes John Arlott's 1949 comment:

Australianism means single-minded determination to win – to win within the laws but, if necessary, to the last limit within them.

That observation was made some sixteen years after the 1932/33 tour, and subsequent events have demonstrated an ever increasing trend in the philosophy he described. This being the case, how did spirit of the game come to be such an Australian priority in the case of leg-theory?

As Jack Hobbs observed, in England the play was as important as the result and schoolboys there had been brought up to absorb the words of Grantland Rice:

For when the One Great Scorer comes
To write against your name,
He marks – not that you won or lost –
But how you played the game.

Had those words been written by one of Australia's cricketing Obergruppenfuhrers, they would more likely have appeared as:

For when the One Great Scorer comes
To see what you have done,
He marks – not how you played the game –
But only if you won.

But Australia hadn't won, and didn't look like winning either. Did this influence the Australian complaint?

THE TIMING OF THE
AUSTRALIAN COMPLAINT

"Moral indignation is merely jealousy with a halo."

H G Wells

"Australians are delightful off a cricket ground, but on most of them lose all sense of proportion. They think they are unbeatable and when defeat comes they cannot stand it."

Jack Hobbs 1933

THE SPARK THAT really ignited what was initially a debate and quickly grew into a furore was the cable dispatched to the MCC by the Australian Board of Control on 18 January 1933. It was sent during the third Test at Adelaide and at a point in that match at which, batting last, Australia faced the mammoth task of having to make 532 runs to win. Having already lost several wickets, defeat was looming.

The Board's cable read:

Bodyline bowling has assumed such proportions as to menace the best interests of the game, making protection of the body by the batsman the main consideration. This is causing intensely bitter feelings between players as well as injury. In our opinion it is unsportsmanlike. Unless stopped at once, it is likely to upset the friendly relations existing between England and Australia.

It would seem the intention of the cable was not solely to lodge a complaint with the MCC but having been released to the press was also designed for local consumption. It would have been better had the Board kept a lid on this at least to begin with because this might have enabled the MCC to consider matters in a more measured light, but knowing that what they had received was public knowledge and included the allegation of being 'unsportsmanlike' put them in a rather different position. It is probable that a contributing reason for the Board's actions was the additional pressure of wagers going down the drain as described in Chapter Four and the Board knew they had to publicly demonstrate that they were at least trying to do something. MCC's response was formal:

> We, Marylebone Cricket Club, deplore your cable. We deprecate your opinion that there has been unsportsmanlike play. We have fullest confidence in captain, team and managers, and are convinced that they do nothing to infringe either the Laws of Cricket or the spirit of the game. We have no evidence that our confidence has been misplaced. Much as we regret accidents to Woodfull and Oldfield, we understand that in neither case was the bowler to blame. If the Australian Board of Control wish to propose a new law or rule it shall receive our careful consideration in due course. We hope the situation is not now as serious as your cable would seem to indicate, but if it is such as to jeopardise the good relations between English and Australian cricketers, and you consider it desirable to cancel remainder of programme, we would consent with great reluctance.

Several days later the Board responded as follows:

> We, Australian Board of Control, appreciate your difficulty in dealing with matter raised in our cable without having seen the

actual play. We unanimously regard bodyline bowling as adopted by some of the games in the present tour as being opposed to the spirit of cricket and unnecessarily dangerous to players. We are deeply concerned that the ideals of the game shall be protected, and have therefore appointed a committee to report on the action necessary to eliminate such bowling from all cricket in Australia as from beginning 1933/34 season.

Will forward copy of committee's recommendation for your consideration, and it is hoped, co-operation, as to its application in all cricket. We do not consider it necessary to cancel remainder of programme.

In stating that they did not feel it necessary to cancel the rest of the program, it is possible the Board now considered that the prospect of losing cash at the turn-styles if the tour was cancelled was of higher priority than the principle they had originally complained about. As Jack Fingleton was to write, most of them were businessmen and MCC seem to have found their Achilles heel.

This exchange was completed by the following MCC cable, saying:

We the Committee of the Marylebone Cricket Club note with pleasure that you do not consider it necessary to cancel the remainder of the programme, and that you are postponing the whole issue involved until after the present tour is completed. May we accept this as a clear indication that the good sportsmanship of our team is not in question? We are sure you will appreciate how impossible it would be to play any Test match in the spirit we all desire unless both sides were satisfied there was no reflection on their sportsmanship. When your recommendation reaches us it shall receive our most careful consideration and will be submitted to the Imperial Cricket Conference.

So much for the cables, but let us consider the underlying reasons for the rumpus. The explosive crowd behaviour at Adelaide has been attributed by others to the blows suffered by Woodfull and Oldfield, neither of which was due to leg-theory, but it is likely that the fuse was lit before the match when Jardine asked that spectators not be allowed into the ground whilst the English team were practising in the nets. Chris Harte's *A History of Australian Cricket* states that the reason for Jardine's request was the number of spectators who turned up to watch on the first day of practice. Harte says this was the first and only time that spectators had been kept out at Adelaide but it seems that it was rather more than the mere number that was the problem. Le Quesne goes a little further to concede that some of the crowd had 'misbehaved themselves' and Frith does actually say that abuse was hurled at Jardine. Talking to Harold Larwood about this episode he said it was far more than just the odd bit of abuse. "At times it was pure bedlam," he said. "You just couldn't even try to conduct a serious practice when you're surrounded by a mob like that making rude and filthy comments every couple of minutes and obviously trying to put us off whether batting or bowling. We were very relieved Mr Jardine did keep them out the next day." And he added, "It wasn't aimed only at Mr Jardine, all of us were all targeted." Asked if an official complaint was lodged Harold admitted he didn't know but said it was certainly warranted. He thought that if one was planned it might have been overtaken by events during the ensuing third Test.

Given that sort of atmosphere it is little wonder that Jardine decided it would be impossible to attempt serious net practice and faced with those circumstances his request appears to have been completely justified. However the Adelaide population and the Press would not have seen things that way and it therefore seems likely that when the match started many of the crowd were already simmering with resentment and were primed to create trouble. If those factors were not enough, when Australia batted, Bradman was dismissed for a paltry 8 runs. The national hero had come up to the country's expectations in the second Test at Melbourne where he made 103 not out in the Australian second innings and, since Australia won that match by 111 runs it could be said that he had largely won it for them and this was what was expected. Now barely two weeks later in Adelaide it was naturally thought he would produce a similar performance. The anticipation and maybe the betting would have been high. It does seem likely that some of the factors provoking the uproar were simmering resentment

Bill Oldfield was forced to retire hurt and unable to bat in the second innings as England won the crucial third Test at Adelaide by 338 runs, sparking the intercontinental furore which follwed.

because spectators had been locked out of the England net practice and disappointment that Bradman had been removed so cheaply. With this anger smouldering away it wouldn't have required much for the flames to take hold.

England had won the first Test quite convincingly, but Australia had been without Bradman. He did return for the second Test and Australia won. So with Bradman once more in the side the series had been squared. Again it is worth noting that there had been no great adverse comment about leg-theory during the second Test. It would seem that with Bradman back, with the Test wins even and three left to play the press, the public and perhaps the Australian Cricket Board felt they did not need to worry about Jardine's leg-theory strategy because it was not going to affect the outcome. Arthur Mailey agreed with this interpretation in his book *Then Came Larwood*. Writing of the second Test, he said:

I had never condemned the leg-theory attack from a sporting angle and had always contended it was legitimate and thoroughly in keeping with the spirit of cricket. But I had expected leg-theory to break down sooner or later because I had faith in Australian batsmen. For this reason I was pleased they had gone so far without making any public "squeak" or complaint.

The pitch for the third Test was much faster than at Melbourne but Australia still persevered with O'Reilly as an opening bowler. Batting first for the only time in the series, England totalled 341, after being 30 for 4 at one point. The Australian innings started just as badly as England's, and early on they were 34 for 3, the batsmen out being Fingleton (0), Bradman (8) and McCabe (also 8). Fingleton was caught at the wicket off Allen and both Bradman and McCabe fell to catches off Larwood. It was shortly after McCabe's dismissal and with Australia in a dire position that a heated affray amongst the crowd occurred when, as Bob Wyatt described it, Woodfull ducked to avoid what he thought was going to be a bouncer but it didn't bounce as expected and struck him on the chest. The pitch was to blame and leg-theory had not even been introduced at that point because the ball was occasionally still swinging away from the batsman. Suddenly, a near-riot broke out and despite what others have written Harold Larwood said he reckoned that whatever Jardine had done would have enraged the crowd even further. "Doing nothing," he said, "was the most sensible course." Later in the same innings and after he had made 41 Oldfield mis-timed a hook shot off Larwood and deflected the ball onto the right side of his temple. He was forced to retire. Later he issued a statement saying the fault was entirely his because he had lost sight of the ball but that was not enough for the press or the crowd at the ground. It might be noted that Oldfield was a right-handed batsman and the ball struck his head on the right side.

Fingleton, Bradman, McCabe, Woodfull and Richardson had been dis-missed some time before Oldfield's injury, and the question that arises is would the same barracking inferno have erupted had Australia been in a stronger position? In other words, had Bradman made his expected runs and instead of the score being 131 for 5 when Oldfield went in to bat, the score had been, say, 331 for 5? The question arises because the anti leg-theory barracking seems to have occurred only when Australia were not faring well. In the event, the English bowling that caused the most trouble for the Australians was not leg-theory but the bowling of Allen who had match figures of 8 for 121. Australia did not bat well in either innings, and England won by the substantial margin of 338 runs.

It was at the closing of the fifth day of the third Test that the Australian Cricket Board appeared to have been pushed into dispatching the aforementioned, somewhat ill-considered cable to Lords to complain that the English bowling tactics were 'unsportsmanlike'. Plain speaking is perhaps a common Australian characteristic, but even so, the wording of that cable was terse. In his book *Cricket Between Two Wars* Plum Warner recounted a conversation he had with an Australian several months later when he said he thought the wording of the first cable was a bit strong and the rejoinder was, "Well, we say what we think." At the Annual General Meeting of the Sussex Club, ex-England captain Arthur Gilligan described the cable as "the roughest, rudest, coarsest cable ever sent from Australia, to which the Marylebone Club had sent a most dignified, courteous and statesmanlike reply". So thoughtless was the wording that even the *Melbourne Herald* was moved to comment:

> The first reaction to the phrase that the continuance of bodyline bowling is likely to upset friendly relations between England and Australia is that it is an hysterical exaggeration. Had the Board added "on the cricket field", Australia would have been saved the derision with which the heavy solemnity of the unfortunate sentence is likely to be received abroad.

From all of this the inference to be drawn seems to be that if Australia had won the third Test or had the Australian position looked favourable on the fifth day, then the cable to Lords would probably not have been sent. This impression seems quite logical unless it could be said that the Board were so embarrassed by the abuse from spectators at the England net practice and the crowd behaviour at Adelaide that they felt they had to make some pre-emptive move to rationalise such behaviour and thus hopefully head off any criticism in that direction. Leading on from this premise, it would seem likely that had Australia then gone on to win the Test series, relatively little would have been heard about leg-theory. The tactic itself would probably have come under some scrutiny, for reasons that will be examined later, but there would probably not have been the fracas that ensued at that time.

Australian cricket writer and commentator, Alan McGilvray, stated that it was only the injuries to Woodfull and Oldfield that prompted the Board complaint. If this is true it should be remembered that leg-theory was responsible for neither of these accidents. If what McGilvray wrote was accurate and he was a man who was fairly close to the source, then it does look as though the Board had been waiting for some specific incident and had used these two occurrences to justify their cable. It also raises the question as to whether there would have been any official Board complaint if these two freak incidents had not occurred. The area that McGilvray does not canvas is whether the massive disappointment in Bradman's cheap dismissal was also a factor.

Allen's public refusal to bowl leg-theory would have played right into the hands of the Australian Board of Control and the press in their attempts to portray leg-theory as unprincipled and outside the 'spirit' of the game. After all, if one of the England 'gentlemen' in the team was so openly against it, then clearly there was some justification for their complaint. Allen's true motives for this position have been examined elsewhere but there can be no doubt he must have been aware his actions were undermining the standing and authority of his captain, Jardine, and the MCC.

Interestingly, in the fourth Test played at Brisbane three weeks after the Adelaide eruption, barracking against England's leg-theory quickly subsided when Woodfull and Richardson put on 133 for the first wicket, an indication perhaps that it was not the principle of leg-theory that was the cause of the outcry, it was the fact of its success. Writing in the *Sydney Sun* on the morning of Monday February 13, as Australia appeared to be in a strong position at the start of the third day's play in the fourth Test, Arthur Mailey said:

The leg-side field in situ at Brisbane, but there were few complaints from the crowd, as noted by Arthur Mailey.

After watching two days of the Brisbane Test I am convinced that cricket has changed with the times, and that fast leg-theory bowling is the aftermath of peace. I mean that no longer will thousands of people sit and watch futile-looking off-side deliveries pass without some outward sign of indignation. On Saturday we had good samples of the much-discussed bodyline bowling, and the more sedate off-theory attack. I should really not call it 'attack', 'compromise' would be a much better word.

On Friday the air was electrical; everybody was on the tip-toe of excitement, waiting for something dramatic to happen. They did not want sedate and apologetic glances between slip fieldsmen; they merely wanted action, something new, something that had a flavour of modernity about it. When Larwood took up the ball to bowl his first over one felt it difficult to suppress a peculiar feeling that comes before every climax. Larwood bowled, and every ball was received with enthusiasm, whether it had been clouted, played with an undesigning bat, or allowed to whistle past without notice.

The introduction of leg-theory has whetted our appetites for something sparkling, virile and risky. Off-theory has had its uses, just as crinolines had, some fifty years ago. Whether we go back to crinolines is matter for the Board of Control.

Leg-theory was outlawed in Australia almost immediately, and it has been suggested that this may have been done in an attempt to force the hand of the MCC. In fact Australia had little option but to take this course of action. It would have laid them open to ridicule if, after complaining so bitterly about this style of bowling, they did nothing to prevent it being used in Australia. Having read or seen at first hand how successful it could be at Test level, what was thought to be leg-theory was now being tried in local matches resulting in injuries being sustained by batsmen from bowlers who really hadn't a clue how to bowl it. Therefore, banning leg-theory was a move the Australian Board had to make and one that was forced on them by their own earlier actions. Despite the Australians saying they would never use this form of attack a form of leg-theory had been tried earlier in Australia. During the 1928/29 tour, according to Jardine's biographer, Christopher Douglas, 'Bull' Alexander became so incensed by Jardine's complaints about his scuffing up the pitch in his follow-through in the MCC match against Victoria, that he resorted to bowling a crude form of leg-theory round the wicket in an attempt to knock Jardine's block off. As Douglas comments, 'It was the height of folly and the result was another Jardine hundred.' One of the Victoria batsmen in that match was Woodfull and no doubt he would have noted this. It has always been denied that Alexander attempted to bowl leg-theory and yet, in a newspaper interview shortly before his death in 1993, Alexander stated that he had indeed tried to hit the English batsmen in the fifth Test; his efforts resulted in match figures of 1 for 154. Given this performance, it is difficult to accept that the addition of any other fast bowler of unreliable accuracy would have produced the desired result. Wild, inaccurate fast bowlers are some of the easiest from which to score runs and moreover if, as Alexander said, he was trying to hit the English batsmen it is difficult to see how he could have done so without bowling on the line of their bodies.

In 2006 the *Daily Telegraph* produced a DVD on the Ashes which included a 2002 Australian Broadcasting Commission documentary on the Bodyline series. In this segment Ian Chappell states that his grandfather, Vic

Richardson had told him Australia did have fast bowlers who could have bowled leg-theory but chose not to use them. Whilst not for one moment doubting that this was what Richardson told his grandson, one has to ask that if there were indeed bowlers of real pace available, then why were they not selected simply as fast bowlers, even ignoring leg-theory? If fast bowlers of Test class existed then why did O'Reilly continue to open the bowling?

Surrounded by the smoke of failure, being devoid of the wherewithal to even attempt a similar tactic and under considerable public pressure, claiming the moral high ground thus appears to have been the only area to which the Australian Cricket Board could retreat.

But desperate though the steps they took may have been, the Board could not have envisaged the way MCC were going to react, the political dimensions that would emerge, nor the search for convenient scapegoats.

THE DEMANDED APOLOGY

"For an Empire builder's duty is by any means to seek
Fresh and up to date improvements in Imperial technique
Now we know that Larwood's bowling may affect the fate of nations
And that leg-traps may imperil our Imperial relations."
The New Statesman & Nation, 1934

Scapegoat : "Person bearing blame that should fall on others."
Oxford English Dictionary

WHILST JARDINE, LARWOOD, Voce & Co were publicly welcomed back to England in 1933 as conquering heroes, there were diplomatic rumblings in the higher echelons of both the MCC and Government due to the planned return of the Australians the very next year in 1934. These rumblings might well be questioned in the light of what has been mentioned earlier, but certainly they deserve examination when people such as Sir Alexander Hore-Ruthven, Jimmy Thomas, and Sir Julian Cahn, plus the MCC, were all involved. Their roles and possible underlying motives are interesting to examine.

Much has been made of the approach to the Dominions Secretary, Jimmy Thomas, by the Governor of South Australia, Hore-Ruthven, early in 1933. Hore-Ruthven was then 60, had held the Governorship since 1928 and like many diplomats before and since, was mainly concerned with maintaining peace in his own bailiwick. Many a diplomat has become closer to

175

Left, Governor of South Australia, Sir Alexander Hore-Ruthven *and, right,*
Dominions Secretary, Jimmy Thomas.

*Hore-Ruthven made appeals to Thomas for the British Government
to intervene. But was he naive? Larwood thought Thomas was the source
of the demanded apology.*

his posting than to his own country. In his attempts to portray the depth of
what he called 'justified local feeling', he told Thomas that in spite of
everything that had occurred, the Australian papers had been very reasonable in their comments. At that time Thomas probably would not have
known any different, but this opinion and description of the local press
relayed to him by Hore-Ruthven flew completely in the face of the views of
the English team and others. They had all said it had been the local papers
that had been primarily responsible for creating the furore that had erupted
- the organs Jack Hobbs had referred to as the 'Yellow Press'. Whether
Hore-Ruthven had actually read any of the Australian press inventions and
exaggerations is not known, but assuming that the man was honest or
believed he was being honest it would seem that he had either read very
selectively or what he was describing to Thomas was merely what had been
relayed to him by others. It certainly did not represent the position on the
ground in Australia. Even that was not enough for Hore-Ruthven, who went

on to claim that leg-theory and barracking were totally different issues and that in any case it was quite unreasonable to expect an indignant crowd of 50,000 to be controlled. He was presumably making a fine distinction between genuine indignation and resentment. Hore-Ruthven had an army background and in the innocent world of the 1930s British military, it would have been unthinkable for a gentleman to suspect anything other than the *prima facie* reason provided. Were the 50,000 crowds quite 'reasonably indignant' at the successes of Richard Hadlee or Muralitharan or even Mike Brearley as referred to in Chapter Two? According to Hore-Ruthven they probably would have been, but then, peace had to be maintained and in the 1930s the English appeared to be masters of appeasement for far more important issues than merely a game of cricket. After all, if Hitler had to be appeased over Czechoslovakia, Ethiopia donated to Mussolini and the Japanese allowed free rein in China, what hope did cricket have?

That Hore-Ruthven genuinely saw his job as keeping his own patch happy is not in doubt and if he used a few exaggerations to obtain his ends he probably felt them to be justified. Whether he thought this to be more important than the rights or wrongs of the matter is not clear but his priorities seem to have been the smooth running of his posting. He even went so far as to suggest that British goods might be at peril and although there does not appear to have been any evidence to support this threat it is unlikely that any politician would have risked it.

Hore-Ruthven no doubt would also have pointed out the involvement of the Australian Prime Minister, J A Lyons, and from the point of view of the Dominions Secretary this must have been evidence enough that the matter had serious diplomatic omens. However, one has to actually live in Australia to understand the totally pivotal position played by sport and the non-stop negative and parochial style of cheap-scoring local politics. Whilst the involvement of the Head of Government would be seen as a significant matter in most countries, in Australia a Prime Minister who ignored such an issue would be pilloried by the Opposition and have the press asking questions at his door. Jimmy Thomas could not have been expected to know this and he would have reacted accordingly.

If solving this problem entailed locating a convenient carpet under which to sweep it or finding some individual to shoulder responsibility, then so be it; the end would justify the means. Hore-Ruthven moved on almost immediately to become Governor of New South Wales and then almost as quickly to be Governor General of Australia. His popularity in Australia may have been partly due to his widely known support for Australia in the leg-theory imbroglio; he became President of MCC in 1948.

Thomas had been Colonial Secretary in the first Labour Government of 1924. In 1930 he became Dominions Secretary in Ramsay MacDonald's controversial National Coalition and as such his office looked after affairs in Australia, Canada, Newfoundland, New Zealand, South Africa and the Irish Free State. It was a post that would normally have been a fairly comfortable cabinet position. Thomas had been born into poverty in Wales and had started work in the railways at the age of 12. He soon became involved in union politics and had organised and led railway strikes in 1911 and 1919. Even by political standards, he does not appear to have been overburdened by scruples and was eventually forced out of politics in 1936 when he was found to have leaked important budget details to certain members of the London Stock Exchange.

Because Ramsay McDonald had always made foreign affairs a personal priority any uncomfortable development in one of the Dominions would have attracted more of his attention than might usually have been expected of a Prime Minister. Although Thomas was perhaps not all that concerned at the happenings in Australia (in any event there does not appear to be any evidence that he had any interest in cricket), he would have been influenced by other cabinet colleagues in the National Government and probably by the Prime Minister himself. A local row over some cricket bowling tactics might not of itself have carried much weight but since there were developments elsewhere in the world at that time that affected vital British interests it could not be viewed in the same isolation that might otherwise have been the case.

1932 had seen the resumption of the Civil Disobedience Movement in India. Mahatma Gandhi was leading salt-march protests, the Indian Congress Party was outlawed and there had been serious Hindu-Moslem riots; early in 1933 the name 'Pakistan' was used for the first time, and Burma was agitating for independence. Amidst considerable opposition (from Churchill for one), debate of The Government of India Bill had begun and the India Office thus had more than its usual share of problems. Over the same period elsewhere in the world the Japanese had occupied the whole of Manchuria and attacked Shanghai where there were considerable British commercial interests and had then withdrawn from the League of Nations. In Europe Hitler had become German Chancellor, the Reichstag had been burned down, De Valera was causing problems in Ireland and in the USA there had been an assassination attempt on President Roosevelt. So the Foreign Office too had plenty to think about.

With all these problems emerging, the last thing the Cabinet of Ramsay MacDonald would have wanted was that some silly argument over a game of cricket in one of its white Dominions should be allowed to fester and explode. There was more than enough to deal with elsewhere. In most cases Empires continued to exist only because of the tacit acceptance of their subject peoples, and this little hiccough had to be kept in place. The Cabinet papers are apparently silent on this matter, but it does not require too much imagination to see that even if he had not already twigged, Thomas was probably told to take whatever steps were necessary to squash the issue and stop a shaky Empire from crumbling even further.

Early in the 1934 cricket season, Harold Larwood was approached by Sir Julian Cahn and told he would have to apologise to MCC for his bowling in Australia and promise to bowl legitimately if he wished to be considered for the coming Test series against Australia. Even 60 years later, Harold was quite adamant that such an ultimatum had indeed been presented to him – very nicely, of course – and that it was Sir Julian who had made the demand. However this method of approach was out of character with the usual style of MCC. Although having an image of being somewhat fusty and establishment, they have not usually been heavy-handed in their method of dealing with problems. Sometimes seen as autocratic and occasionally misguided, they have generally acted honourably and in what they have believed to be the best overall interests of the game. There have been times when they have taken action if they felt a player had stepped out of line, but to have demanded that Larwood provide a written undertaking to refrain from a certain method of attack smacked of the intervention of another party. If MCC wanted Larwood to ensure that he would not bowl leg-theory then all they had to do was to give the appropriate directions to whoever was captaining the Test team. Larwood was a professional and would have had to follow the captain's instructions and if he didn't, he would simply have been taken off and not selected for the next match. It did not require any undertaking written or otherwise, and that this was demanded points to the source being other than MCC.

Moreover if MCC had required such an undertaking it would have been tantamount to conceding that without such a document they had no control over the professional players. That would have set a very uncomfortable precedent. It was also incongruous for the required apology to have come solely from within MCC. They knew that the tactics used during the 1932/33 Australian tour had been developed by the team under their appointed captain Jardine, and they knew that Larwood was merely the weapon. The manner in which his bowling was directed was out of his hands. Four fast bowlers had been selected for that series, plus the fast-medium Maurice Tate, so the selection of the bowling attack had deliberately concentrated on pace at the outset. Moreover they knew that all they needed to do to mollify the Australians was to direct that leg-theory not be bowled. Perhaps the most telling indication was the fact that although Larwood had been told he must apologise to MCC, nobody apparently thought to enquire whether it was MCC itself that had made this demand. Asked about this aspect in the 1990s, Harold said that the question had not occurred to him at the time and he had not asked. He had been told he must apologise to MCC and he had therefore assumed the message must have come from them. A written apology and the mystery surrounding the source could smack of the intervention of a politician who could wave a piece of paper to demonstrate what he had achieved. Clearly, the demand could not be for an apology to the Government and to say sorry to Australia would have aroused considerable public reaction, but apologise to MCC? Now that would have been a different matter.

The then President of MCC Lord Hailsham described allegations of Thomas's influence as "the most extraordinary moonshine" and considering that Thomas had no apparent connection with Cahn he may have believed this to be true. Hailsham would probably have not wanted to concede any political influence let alone from the Labour Party, but if political involvement was indeed the 'moonshine' he claimed it to be then it is strange that

Hailsham did not specifically state either that it had indeed been MCC who had made the demand or it was not MCC; this is what one might have expected if no other party was actually responsible. The whole imbroglio had a suspicious odour about it. A further element that threw doubt on the source having been MCC was the question of what would MCC have done with such a document, anyway? As has been demonstrated, MCC didn't need any document promising or apologising for anything to ensure that a County professional toed the line. The popular press would have had a field day and MCC would have been made a laughing stock. However, if Thomas was not behind it then the alternative and perhaps more likely source was Sir Julian Cahn himself.

Cahn was a man of considerable wealth accumulated by cleverly expanding a furniture business that he had inherited from his father through the introduction of hire purchase. Like many a self-made man of that era in the UK, he had social aspirations and craved entry to the landed establishment and even the aristocracy. Cahn had been born in 1883 and by 1933 at the age of 50 had acquired a baronetcy through shrewd use and discriminating dispersal of the funds at his disposal and had become a cricket fanatic. He had created two cricket grounds of his own where he organised high-standard matches featuring his own teams. He had been accepted as a Member of the MCC but had further ambitions to be elected to one of their Committees. In this he was not successful. Whether this was because he was in 'trade', a dirty word amongst the establishment then and for some years to come, or that he was Jewish, or that he was really only a nouveaux riche foreigner, is not known. The English can be remarkably stubborn on some matters, as the present owner of Harrods has discovered.

This frustration was not one that could be overcome financially as in many other areas where Cahn had had ambitions or desires. However if he could persuade Larwood to sign his demanded apology, then perhaps he could demonstrate his influence to MCC and gain entry to its hallowed higher echelons that he so desperately craved. He could say he'd had a word with Larwood and he could then demonstrate his powers of persuasion by getting him to complete the apology that he, Cahn, had drafted. All these possibilities and conjectures were bounced around at the time, but the final word lay with Harold Larwood himself. In his own book he says that Arthur Carr had later told him that the source of the demanded apology was Jimmy Thomas and that Cahn was merely the intermediary. Asked again in the 1990s Harold was adamant that Carr had indeed told him this was the case. It does make more sense than anything else. Thomas, devious politician though he was, apparently had little understanding of cricket or cricketers and does not appear to have realised that in trying to bolster his own position he was only adding fuel to the already smouldering problem. Larwood said later that he'd had just about enough. He had already been approached for a comment by the *Sunday Dispatch*, and an article appeared under his name in which he said he was finished with Test cricket for good. He undoubtedly felt provoked – whether the article was the wisest move is another thing – but detached judgment and retrospective knowledge were advantages he did not have; it is always easier to be wise after the event.

Warner later said that had the article not appeared, Larwood was indeed on the selectors' list. This may or may not be true but unfortunately no records seem to have survived. What can be said is that it is a convenient way to explain why Larwood was not chosen and it puts the blame on him rather than having questions asked of the Selection Committee and, of course, Warner himself was one of the Selectors.

As for Voce, it is said that he made some sort of apology but there does not appear to be any evidence that this was actually in writing. In any event, verbal or not, it was an uncalled-for humiliation of an honest man, but professionals were still merely gardeners, grooms and gamekeepers in some eyes. Allen is also said to have demanded that Voce make this gesture if he wanted to be included in his 1936/37 touring side. Asked about this, Harold Larwood merely said, "Well, you know, Bill was five years younger than me, so he had more to lose. I have my own views about Allen, but I don't blame Bill at all for going along with it." As it turned out, Voce was by far the most successful of the England bowlers in the 1936/37 series, so Allen seems to have got the striker he wanted but on terms that would have kept him popular with all his Australian friends. However, for poor Voce, the five-year advantage was to disappear during the five years of World War II. As we shall see later, Voce only made the gesture to keep his career going and not because he genuinely felt any regret.

It must be asked why were apologies, from whatever source, demanded only from two professionals and not at least some explanation from Jardine, if indeed any explanation was warranted. After all Jardine had been in charge of the side selected for him and had directed operations. There is one possible and quite probable reason. Douglas Jardine, not being dependent upon playing cricket for his livelihood and knowing precisely what had transpired within Lords, had politely told them to 'get stuffed', or words to that effect. It is entirely reasonable that the Selection Committee, having chosen five fast bowlers in the first place, did in fact say to Jardine, "We've given you the ammunition; use it as you wish, but bring back the Ashes", and now under some political pressure wanted to back away from that position. If questioned, Jardine may well have just thrown this back in their faces and possibly publicly said, "You asked me to regain the Ashes; I've done so and have stayed completely within the rules. Now you are moralising on matters of detail because of outside pressure." Better, therefore, to let sleeping dogs lie, keep a lid on the matter and, in particular, keep things out of the public eye.

Because no published explanation was ever requested of Jardine, what emerged from all of this appears to have been a quasi-solution that was entirely political and had little to do with either cricket or moral issues. It was dishonourable but political establishments have rarely had any interest in principles. Finding a likely solution was necessary and if this involved offering up some sacrificial lamb then so be it. Once again as in the case of Hore-Ruthven the end would justify the means. It may seem Anglophobic but there are times when the expression 'Perfidious Albion' is understandable. In all of this, MCC appear to have acted almost as an extension of the Dominions Office. Their readiness to appease for the sake of political peace may have re-appeared in the West Indies in 1980-81. In that series Robin Jackman the leading County Cricket wicket-taker in 1980 was refused entry by the left-wing Government of Guiana because he had played in South Africa. Faced with this sort of political grandstanding, MCC could have told the West Indian Board of Control that they assumed the tour was being called off. Of course, this would really have set the cat amongst the West Indian pigeons, yet it might have induced a re-think. Instead 'talks' were undertaken, which resulted in a compromise: the Georgetown Test was cancelled, but the remainder of the series continued. How much of the influence on that issue was Westminster rather than Lords - just as it seems to have been in 1934? As an additional ingredient to this murky mixture of intrigue, MCC records for the period concerned appear to have been consigned to the dustbin in what has been described as an 'economy measure' during World War II. It may be thought that this was nothing more than an unfortunate administrative oversight except for the fact that throughout the War period the MCC Deputy Secretary was Pelham Warner himself. Had he made sure that such an 'economy measure' removed the possibility of anything embarrassing being available for future scrutiny? After all, just what was the economy?

But to get back to Jardine, whether he was or was not justified, was of minor importance when compared with the need to pacify a part of an increasingly independent Empire. Cricket was nothing more than a small part on this chessboard. Jardine could not be touched, but mere technicians such as Larwood and Voce could be shifted around and handled like pawns.

And there was more to come.

BANNING OF LEG THEORY

"What was good and fair for Bradman could not possibly be
served up to our thoroughbred English gentlemen."
Neville Cardus, 1934

"I for one will always regret that legislation was introduced to stop that
type of attack instead of allowing events to take their normal course."
Bill Bowes, 1949

THE AUSTRALIANS ACTED swiftly to outlaw leg-theory soon after the
conclusion of the 1932/33 tour and in this they really had no option but to
take such action, given their own much publicised complaints.

There were other problems in Australia that undoubtedly influenced
the Board in their decision. The vast majority of the Australian cricket-
playing community had never witnessed leg-theory at first hand, and there
was a total misconception of what it really was. Because of the colourful
and distorted accounts that appeared in the local press, young boys and
men playing Grade cricket were being injured by bowlers aiming at
batsmen's heads in the belief that what they were bowling was leg-theory.
It was not leg-theory, of course, but such had been the exaggerations
appearing in the Australian papers and the clear success of the tactic that
bowlers all over the country were trying to emulate a style of bowling
without understanding it, under the impression that this was what leg-
theory was all about

In England, things moved more slowly. At first there was little concern and the general thought was that Australia had over-reacted. This view gradually changed with the passionate remonstrations of Hore-Ruthven to the Dominions Secretary and the approach of the 1934 season. The planned visitors were the Australians again, but they had indicated that without a prior undertaking that leg-theory would not be employed, the tour would not go ahead. Here again, the Australians had, unwittingly perhaps, created a situation whereby they had to demand such an undertaking because of their earlier complaints and moreover they had to obtain some assurance before they boarded ship otherwise they could have arrived in England and found themselves having to deal with the same attack all over again, and in those days, they couldn't just get the next plane home. Although the Australians found themselves in a corner of their own making, their ultimatum did force the authorities in England to rethink the issue. MCC did not want the coming Australian tour to be abandoned and so, although not actually providing the requested undertaking, they said they would do their best to ensure that the Australians had an enjoyable tour. This seems to have mollified the Australians and with that gesture they agreed to arrive as planned. What is not generally known is just how close the MCC Committee came to telling the Australians that perhaps they might find it better if they stayed at home which really would have upset the applecart. The Committee vote not to take this action was only eight to five.

In addition to the financial loss that would be suffered if the Australians did not tour, there was another factor that appears to have remained largely unexplored. Leg-theory would have made the game particularly uncomfortable for the amateurs because for the most part, the amateurs in charge of the County game in England at that time were batsmen, of some sort at least, with only a few medium-paced bowlers, let alone fast bowlers. Admittedly Farnes was just emerging but he was one of the exceptions. Allen, an amateur fast bowler, having so publicly stated his refusal to bowl leg theory, would be counted on to join the anti-leg-theory lobby (his reasons for this position have been discussed elsewhere), but the remainder of the fast bowlers in England were mainly professionals and, although their interests were very much involved, it seems that not one of them was asked their opinion.

Within the position of the amateur and the establishment control of County cricket there were quite a number who would have played little constructive part in any County's performance or success. A crucial aspect though, when leg-theory is considered, is that all of them played cricket not because it provided them with a living, as it did the professionals, but because they enjoyed it. It was a very pleasant pastime and carried with it a degree of social prestige. Very rarely did a professional fast bowler deliver bouncers at an amateur batsman because it would have been considered akin to tripping up an old lady with an umbrella or saying 'balls' to the Colonel – for the 'play' was as important as the result. If not controlled, leg-theory would have produced a position whereby this pastime was decidedly uncomfortable at times. Therefore, it seems highly likely that this aspect and the views and opinions of the gentleman cricketer would have been extremely influential. On English pitches leg-theory would not have pre-sented the same problem as it had on the faster harder pitches in Australia and in most cases the bounce would have been far more consistent. Nonetheless, it would not have been comfortable. This position was summed up by Neville Cardus in his essay on Harold Larwood published in *The Playfair*. He wrote that 'what was good and fair for Bradman could not possibly be served up to our own thoroughbred gentlemen'. It should be remembered, too, that it was a very 'thoroughbred English gentleman', the Hon. Freddie Calthorpe, who launched Bill Voce at the West Indies in 1930 and then complained that Constantine's similar leg-side attack was 'not cricket'. Politically, it could not be admitted that the position of the amateur was a consideration as even in the mid-1930s, it would have pro-voked considerable reaction if the public realised that the ruling elite were so carefully looking after their own. Jardine had shown during the West Indies Tests of 1933 that he could play leg-theory without a problem but he was the exception amongst the amateurs.

Bowling fast is a physically demanding way of earning a living, so it is probably not surprising that this job was mostly left to the professionals, but the professionals do not appear to have been consulted about the banning of leg-theory. It is reasonable to assume that there would have been varying opinions amongst the professional batsmen anyway and some, like Sutcliffe, might have said they had no problem with leg-theory whilst others, perhaps the less fleet of foot, would have voted against it. What would have been the majority view of the County fast bowlers whose sweat and perseverance were being worn out on batsmen's wickets with an LBW law that favoured the batsman? Would most of them have said no? We will never know but it is probably safe to assume that there would have been a mixed response with some supporting the change and others saying they saw nothing wrong with it. However, what we do know is that none of them were asked.

Bill Bowes, Yorkshire and England fast bowler and later a successful and respected journalist, said of leg-theory that he felt a new technique was required by batsmen at that stage of cricket development and that as with every style of delivery the bowler produced, it was only a matter of time before batsmen would find a perfect counter. He regretted that legislation was introduced to stop that style of attack instead of allowing events to take their normal course. Bowes may have been right but the imminent arrival of the 1934 Australians meant that events could not be allowed to take their normal course but this might have taken several years to unfold and with the Australians demanding undertakings prior to their arrival, decisions had to be made to put things in order – rightly or wrongly.

A situation thus emerged similar to that in Australia. Having complained so bitterly and emotionally about leg-theory, the Australian cricket authorities were forced to outlaw the tactic in their country and having then requested MCC to provide a prior undertaking that leg-theory would not be used during their coming tour of England, they had unwittingly forced the MCC to make a similar ruling for County cricket and if this had not been done, a situation would have arisen whereby leg-theory was acceptable at one level but banned at another. Quite clearly, the same rules had to apply throughout English cricket and so, one thing leading almost accidentally to another, by the beginning of the 1934 English season a set of circumstances had come about that had not been envisaged when the Australians complained after the third Test at Adelaide a year earlier. As with other aspects of this fracas what had been intended originally as little more than a protest (perhaps provoked by Australian defeats), had gradually gathered momentum and exploded into something of a major international cricket issue.

There was, however, a further domestic perspective to all this. A number of complaints had come from certain Counties about the leg-theory being practised by Nottinghamshire and as was the case in Australia those protests came from Counties who did not possess bowlers of real pace. That Larwood could bowl leg-theory elsewhere was accepted but apparently not in County cricket with the result that howls of protest were now heard whenever a bowler dropped one short. Leg-theory bowled in Australia was assisted by lightning-fast pitches and unpredictable bounce, whereas a fast bowler in England had to 'dig it in' and bowl really short to get the ball to rise. To the spectator such bowling was thus far more obviously intimidating than the leg-theory bowled in Australia and even if not so in fact, it would have looked dangerous.

Along with complaints about Larwood came some about Voce as well, which considering he was a left-arm bowler whose natural swing was into the right-handed batsman, seems unreasonable. A leg-side field must surely have been just as fair and natural for a fast left-handed bowler as a string of slips was for a right-handed fast bowler. This was a point emphasised by Harold Larwood himself in 1993: the furore was such that nobody seemed capable of telling the difference. It was a point also picked up by Neville Cardus who said in 1934 that Voce could as legitimately bowl to his four legs as Larwood could bowl to his four slips. A degree of hysteria seems to have broken loose, and poor Voce found his natural advantage being held against him. Of course, he was a professional and would be expected to accept this unreasonable restraint 'like a good chap'. Much of the anti-Voce chorus appears to have emanated from the Australian team and their 1934 match against Notts. Voce did not bowl leg-theory in that match; he bowled as he had in County cricket for some years. Perhaps it was simply his height of 6 foot 3 that caused the Australian complaints as he took 8 for 66. Were the Australians still carrying ghosts with them, or did they feel they could maintain the momentum that had gathered?

The anti-anything-short-because-it-might-be-leg-theory bandwagon gathered such pace that when playing the Australians at Lords, Bill Bowes says a note was sent from the pavilion to the England captain, Wyatt, which read: 'Ask Bowes not to bowl short'. When Bowes asked Wyatt what his response was to be, he was told, "Well, if they want it friendly, perhaps they'd better have it that way." So worried apparently were MCC that anything that could be remotely interpreted as leg-theory was quietly prohibited. Even the occasional bouncer was outlawed in an effort to appease the sensitive visitors. The command came to produce 'friendly' bowling.

One beneficial outcome did result for the toiling professional bowler, however. It was tacitly accepted that leg-theory had evolved because laws and wickets overwhelmingly favoured the batsman, and calls came for some move to be made to provide a more even contest between bat and ball. Consequently, the LBW law was amended to allow a dismissal to a ball pitched outside the off stump, thus bringing to an end the imperious manner in which batsmen had been calmly using their pads to protect their wickets from any delivery not pitched in line with the stumps. A compromise solution had been found, and one that seemed to ensure, as far as possible, that the game continued as before. Yet, as is so often the case with compromises, it did not fully address the situation and only postponed the issue and redirected the problem. Jack Fingleton speculated thus in *Cricket Crisis* when he wrote:

> Had not War intervened I often wonder what would have been Hutton's experience had that 1940/41 tour eventuated and had he set about emulating Bradman's big deeds. I do not think any prim compromise between the Board and the MCC would have stopped fast bowlers from exploiting the theory that Hutton did not like bumpers. And would the Australian crowds the have shouted "bodyline" against their own bowlers?

In 1946/47 England were faced with a very hostile pair of fast bowlers in Lindwall and Miller, who unleashed a barrage of brutal bouncers at the English batting. This onslaught continued in 1948 when Denis Compton sustained a far worse head injury from a Lindwall bouncer than anything suffered by the Australians from leg-theory.

As for Australia in 1932/33, just after World War II England did not possess bowlers fast enough to respond in like fashion. If there had been a genuine reason for the earlier Australian complaint about leg-theory, one would think that a similar English protest would have been justified. Plum Warner does make reference to this in his biography *Long Innings* when talking of 'Bodyline'. He says:

The curious and ironical consequence was that in 1948 this country saw a recurrence of it by, of all people, the Australians themselves – Bradman's famous team – who had been so bitterly antagonistic to it. At Trent Bridge, in the first Test, Miller, as *The Times* put it, "with a toss of his mane and a petulant mien, gave the impression that intimidation was at least part of his object", and at Old Trafford in the third Test there was a good deal of unpleasantness. Private conversation between the authorities subsequently put matters on a calmer basis.

Just how MCC made their point is not known but it may have involved some reference back to the Australian complaints in 1932/33. In any event it was handled quietly and out of the public arena. Had the Australians been on the receiving end, it would be interesting to know what their response might have been. In many ways leg-theory was less dangerous because the batsman knew exactly what to expect; the danger in the sudden very fast bouncer was that it could not be predicted. Bouncers are intended to be hostile and intimidating rather than wicket-taking because the fast-footed and quick-thinking batsman only needs to duck and there should be no chance of losing his wicket. As has so often been the case, though, it is the losing side that complains.

What seems to have emerged from the skulduggery of this murky scenario? The powers that be chose a path that was smooth rather than one that was honest. It was a case of retrospective moralising to accommodate political pressure and we might ask: just how many of the attacks on Jardine were actually designed to deflect attention from questions elsewhere?

There is one interesting footnote to all of this. Just over 12 months separated the end of the 1932/33 Australian season and the arrival of the Australians in England for their 1934 tour, therefore if matters were to move at all, they had to move fairly quickly. But what might have happened had Australia been scheduled to tour a year later?

Naturally this is speculation, but had the scheduled 1934 tourists been South Africa, would they have made any demands about leg-theory before setting foot on English soil? We cannot be certain, of course, but probably not. Without the urgency imposed by this time frame, would the silly demand for an apology from Harold Larwood have been made at all? Moreover, if the MCC had had the time to consider matters in a more leisurely manner, would the result have been the type of solution suggested by Bill Bowes? And perhaps, just perhaps, Harold Larwood and Douglas Jardine would not have been hung out to dry on the clothesline of political expediency.

Asked in the 1990s whether he thought it was as much the timing as the 'principle' that had been the prime factor, Harold merely chuckled quietly and said, "Yes, well maybe, but what happened, happened, and you know, you can't change history."

What a pity we can't.

IMPLICATIONS, INFERENCES, CONCLUSIONS?

"I have a feeling that if Larwood and leg-theory had been
Australian the crowds there would have laughed and
applauded had our men been discomforted."

Jack Hobbs, 1933

"I think, looking back, the Australians made too much fuss about it."

Jack Fingleton, 1977

MOST OF THE influences, issues and cultural aspects already discussed
have been left untouched in earlier accounts of the 1932/33 events. This
book has put forward various elements for consideration, but it should not
be thought that anything is being presented as established fact. One can
draw fairly rational inferences, however, and maybe from those some
conclusions as to probable underlying truths. A number of matters throw
considerable doubts on the conventional view of what was really behind
what transpired during that tour and why various parties acted and
responded in the way they did.

In Australia decades of repeated brainwashing about the evils of 'bodyline' has resulted in an orthodox mantra that, like a Latin mass, is repeated
even though not understood. It seems to have become conventional to paint
Douglas Jardine as the snobbish, aloof, cold-hearted architect and execu-
tioner of leg-theory, and the Australians as the hapless victims. There is no

doubt that he was not an easy man to get to know, apparently due in part to the shyness described by Harold Larwood, but does that justify the vilification to which he was subjected in Australia? Had Australia won that series, would anyone have put Jardine's personality under the microscope? And again, if he was such a martinet, the stern and detached commander that some have alleged, why did the whole team club together to present him with the silver cigar box?

The problem does not appear to have been Douglas Jardine, but the culture he had unwittingly stirred up. It was a fragile isolated society that tended to react and respond like a wounded bear and it does look as though his alleged personality may largely have been milked simply to legitimise the Australian reaction. It has also been said that Jardine was the 'wrong man' to send to Australia, that the Australians would not 'like' him. This is an interesting point of view, but if it is to be considered at all, then also to be asked is whether the Australians have thought some of their own choices were the 'right' men for England. It would be interesting to know just what the hierarchy at Lord's really thought of Warwick Armstrong or the overt sledging tactics of Allan Border. Why, it must be asked, did England have to consider Australia if the reverse did not also apply?

Harold Larwood's role has been microscopically examined many times, however, even 60 years later, Harold said he couldn't see that leg-theory was unfair and, although he was personally pilloried over it, he was quite philosophical about it. Interestingly, he also said that in his last meeting in England with Bill Voce, Voce had confided in him that he had only made the comments about regretting leg-theory "to get them off my back and get on with playing cricket". He had added, "There was now't wrong with it, they just couldn't handle it, that's all". Voce may not have been willing to state this view publicly but it is one of the missing pieces of the jigsaw now filled in by Harold Larwood himself.

How much pressure was exerted behind the scenes by the British Government and if MCC were indeed leant on, how much of the need to keep a lid on things was influenced by world affairs as a whole at that time? In 1949 MCC invited Harold Larwood to become an honorary member and although 15 years after the event, was this overdue gesture a tacit admission that he had indeed been made the scapegoat? At the age of 88 Larwood was awarded an MBE at the personal instigation of British Prime Minister, John Major. Major was a cricket fan, but it was a long overdue gesture and possibly an implied admission that the Government had indeed been an influential factor in the treatment meted out to him in the aftermath of the 1932/33 series. Would John Major have made a similar gesture to Douglas Jardine? Jardine had been dead some 35 years by then, but had he still been alive, would some similar recognition been accorded to him? What might Stan McCabe's handling of leg-theory have been had he not continued to play with an increasingly debilitating illness, and to what extent were Australia's performances hampered by what seem to have been a series of blunders by the Australian selectors? To what extent were the problems Australia was facing made far worse by selection bungling coupled with religious and racial discrimination? Violence and demonstrations are regular features of the Australian landscape but how much of cricket crowd fury was the result of betting and lost wagers? And did alcohol play a part, or was one of the main culprits the Australian press in whipping up the anti-Jardine furore? Pitches of unpredictable bounce were specifically mentioned by Larwood, Voce and Allen; to what extent did this factor assist in making leg-theory even more difficult to handle? Not surprisingly perhaps, this aspect has never been mentioned by the Australians who may have been reluctant to concede that it was their own pitches that were contributing to the problems they were facing.

The previous MCC tours of 1924/25 and 1928/29 had taken place at a time of prosperity and rapid growth in Australia but by the time Jardine's side arrived in 1932, the social and economic picture had changed dramatically and England was seen as having contributed to the hardship brought about by the Great Depression. Given these facts, how much of the Australian reaction was due to these outside issues, which had largely evaporated by the time Allen's side arrived in 1936?

Allen's publicly stated refusal to bowl leg-theory appears to have been accepted in many quarters as an indication of his moral backbone in the face of Jardine's strategy. Allen never ventured into formal print himself on the series, no doubt hoping that his pronouncements during the tour would obtain the required interpretation, and he largely achieved this objective when he collaborated with Swanton in the book *Gubby Allen - Man of*

Cricket. Although that book does contain a few extracts from his letters it is not clear whether these were picked by Swanton, or selected for release by Allen himself. In any event, the letters quoted present only a portion of the whole picture more recently revealed by Brian Rendell.

Plum Warner was later knighted for 'services to cricket'. But just how much were his services to the British Government also behind this award. The conventional image of a cricketing missionary becomes slightly obscure with deeper investigation. He did however produce the following tribute following Jardine's death in 1958:

> In my humble opinion, Jardine was a very fine captain, both on and off the field, and in the committee-room he was also extremely good. If ever there was a cricket match between England and the rest of the world and the fate of England depended on its result, I would pick Jardine as England captain every time.

When Warner mentioned the rest of the world, presumably he was including Australia.

What really would have been Australia's reaction if they had had at their disposal a bowler of genuine, accurate pace? Would they have used such a bowler in the same way and if they did have bowlers of genuine pace then why were none of them selected, even without trying leg-theory? Had Australia been able to master leg-theory and emerged victorious, would the reaction have been little more than 'Well, they tried this bodyline stuff, but it didn't get them anywhere'? Indeed would there have been any such reaction in a country where sport was not the cultural religion?

Larwood and Voce were to be badly missed in 1934, the English selectors shuffling their cards of Bowes, Farnes, Clark, Geary and Allen in an effort to fill their shoes. Not one of these played in all of the Tests and between them the five bowlers managed just 46 wickets in the five Test series, at an average of 35. Allen's bowling average was 73. By comparison, the pair of Larwood and Voce had taken 48 wickets in 1932/33 at an average of 22, and at least 70 per cent of those wickets were not due to leg-theory. Peace had been bought, but at what moral cost? It seems to have been a case of hypocrisy all round. And to put the matter into a wider, historical perspective, as a fast bowling strategy leg-theory does not compare at all unfavourably with what was to emerge soon after World War II with the barrage of brutal bumpers delivered by Lindwall and Miller and then Lillee and Thomson. When the speed weapon was available Australia used it without mercy as they had done earlier through McDonald and Gregory. When comment was made about his shock tactics, the terse retort from Bradman in 1947 was, "They've got a bat, haven't they?" This was the same Bradman who used pious innocence when he pointed the finger at Harold Larwood. Didn't the Australians of 1932/33 have any bats? The crucial although perhaps uneasy question to be asked must be whether there would have been any complaint had Australia emerged victorious and Bradman had continued his previous dominating performances?

Jardine behaved with great dignity under enormous pressure and provocation, and did not for one moment betray any confidences, for which MCC should have been very grateful. Just a few revelations might have caused massive embarrassment. Some forty years later, Surrey's famed captain, Percy Fender, was one of the few who had the courage to put matters into a realistic perspective. Writing of the 1932/33 tour, he said:

> For the first time in my career, England had appointed a determined and resolute captain, a man cast in the toughest Australian mould, a la Armstrong if you like, and what happened? It all went wrong and was followed by the climb down when the Counties thought the 1934 Australian visit was in jeopardy.

Today Douglas Jardine might have been knighted and instead of having to emigrate, Harold Larwood would have continued as a national hero. Both men were individuals of courage and integrity.

The 1995 Memorial Service for Harold Larwood included the following lines by Ellen Brenneman:

> And think of him as living
> In the hearts of those he touched
> For nothing loved is ever lost
> And he was loved so much.

Both these men should have been celebrated then and admired now. They were treated in a shabby fashion in England for political reasons by an equivocal establishment for merely doing their best for their country. The names of those who conspired against them have sunk from sight. Their own names will endure far longer.

Left, Douglas Jardine and, right, Harold Larwood.
Two men who will forever be synonymous with Bodyline, but for whom history has shone a very unfair light on their contributions to that infamous series.

APPENDICES:
SCORECARDS & AVERAGES
FOR THE 1932/33 SERIES

First Test, Sydney – England won by 10 wickets
2, 3, 5, 6, 7 December 1932   Umpires: G. Borwick and G.A. Hele

Australia

Woodfull	c Ames	b Voce	7		b Larwood	0
Ponsford		b Larwood	32		b Voce	2
Fingleton	c Allen	b Larwood	26	c Voce	b Larwood	40
Kippax	lbw	b Larwood	8		b Larwood	19
McCabe	not out		187	lbw	b Hammond	32
Richardson	c Hammond	b Voce	49	c Voce	b Hammond	0
Oldfield	c Ames	b Larwood	4	c Leyland	b Larwood	1
Grimmett	c Ames	b Voce	19	c Allen	b Larwood	1
Nagel		b Larwood	0	not out		21
O'Reilly		b Voce	4		b Voce	7
Wall	c Allen	b Hammond	4	c Ames	b Allen	2
	Byes 12, lb 4, nb 4		20	Byes 12, lb 2, w 1, nb 2		17
	Total		360	Total		164

FOW 1st: 22, 65, 82, 87, 216, 251, 299, 300, 305   2nd: 2, 10, 61, 61, 100, 104, 105, 115, 151

	O	M	R	W	O	M	R	W
Larwood	51	5	96	5	18	4	28	5
Voce	29	4	110	4	17.5	5	54	2
Allen	15	1	65	0	9	5	15	1
Verity	15	4	55	0	4	1	15	0
Hammond	14.2	0	54	1	15	6	37	2

England

Sutcliffe	lbw	b Wall	194	not out	1
Wyatt	lbw	b Grimmett	38	not out	0
Hammond	c Grimmett	b Nagel	112		
Pataudi		b Nagel	102		
Leyland	c Oldfield	b Wall	0		
Jardine	c Oldfield	b McCabe	27		
Verity	lbw	b Wall	2		
Allen	c and	b O'Reilly	19		
Ames	c McCabe	b O'Reilly	0		
Larwood	lbw	b O'Reilly	0		
Voce	not out		0		
	Byes 7, lb 17, nb 6		50		
	Total		524	Total	1

FOW 1st: 112, 300, 425, 425, 470, 479, 518, 522, 522, 524

	O	M	R	W	O	M	R	W
Wall	38	4	104	3				
Nagel	43.4	9	110	2				
O'Reilly	67	32	117	3				
Grimmett	64	22	118	1				
McCabe	15	2	42	1	0.1	0	1	0
Kippax	2	1	5	0				

Second Test, Melbourne – Australia won by 111 runs
30, 31 December 1932 & 2, 3 January 1933
Umpires: G. Borwick and G.A. Hele

Australia

Fingleton		b Allen	85	c Ames	b Allen	1
Woodfull		b Allen	10	c Allen	b Larwood	26
O'Brien	run out		10		b Larwood	11
Bradman		b Bowes	0	not out		103
McCabe	c Jardine	b Voce	32		b Allen	0
Richardson	c Hammond	b Voce	34	lbw	b Hammond	32
Oldfield	not out		27		b Voce	6
Grimmett	c Sutcliffe	b Voce	2		b Voce	0
Wall	run out		1	lbw	b Hammond	3
O'Reilly		b Larwood	15	c Ames	b Hammond	0
Ironmonger		b Larwood	4	run out		0
	Byes 5, lb 1, w 2, nb 2		10	Byes 5, lb 1, w 4, nb 1		9
	Total		228	Total		191

FOW 1st: 29, 67, 67, 151, 156, 188, 194, 200, 222   2nd: 21, 27, 78, 81, 135, 150, 156, 184, 186

	O	M	R	W	O	M	R	W
Larwood	20.5	2	52	2	15	2	50	2
Voce	20	3	54	3	15	2	47	2
Allen	17	3	41	2	12	1	44	2
Hammond	10	3	21	0	10.5	2	21	5
Bowes	19	2	50	1	4	0	20	0

England

Sutcliffe	c Richardson	b Wall	52		b O'Reilly	33
Wyatt	lbw	b O'Reilly	13	lbw	b O'Reilly	25
Hammond		b Wall	8	c O'Brien	b O'Reilly	23
Pataudi		b O'Reilly	15	c Fingleton	b Ironmonger	5
Leyland		b O'Reilly	22		b Wall	19
Jardine	c Oldfield	b Wall	1	c McCabe	b Ironmonger	0
Ames		b Wall	4	c Fingleton	b O'Reilly	2
Allen	c Richardson	b O'Reilly	30	st Oldfield	b Ironmonger	23
Larwood		b O'Reilly	9	c Wall	b Ironmonger	4
Voce	c McCabe	b Grimmett	6	c O'Brien	b O'Reilly	0
Bowes	not out		4	not out		0
	Byes 1, lb 2, nb 2		5	lb 4, nb 1		5
	Total		169	Total		139

FOW 1st: 30, 43, 83, 98, 104, 110, 122, 138, 161   2nd: 53, 55, 70, 70, 77, 85, 135, 137, 138

	O	M	R	W	O	M	R	W
Wall	21	4	52	4	8	2	25	1
O'Reilly	34.3	17	63	5	24	5	66	5
Grimmett	16	4	21	1	4	0	19	0
Ironmonger	14	4	28	0	19.1	8	26	4

Third Test, Adelaide – England won by 338 runs
13, 14, 16, 17, 18, 19 January 1933   Umpires: G. Borwick and G.A. Hele

England

Batsman	1st innings	R	2nd innings	R
Sutcliffe	c Wall b O'Reilly	9	c sub (O'Brien) b Wall	7
Jardine	b Wall	3	lbw b Ironmonger	56
Hammond	c Oldfield b Wall	2	b Bradman	85
Ames	b Ironmonger	3	b O'Reilly	69
Leyland	b O'Reilly	83	c Wall b Ironmonger	42
Wyatt	c Richardson b Grimmett	78	c Wall b O'Reilly	49
Paynter	c Fingleton b Wall	77	not out	1
Allen	lbw b Grimmett	15	lbw b Grimmett	15
Verity	c Richardson b Wall	45	lbw b O'Reilly	40
Voce	b Wall	8	b O'Reilly	8
Larwood	not out	3	c Bradman b Ironmonger	8
Extras	Byes 1, lb 7, nb 7	15	b 17, lb 11, nb 4	32
Total		**341**		**412**

FOW 1st: 4, 16, 16, 30, 186, 196, 228, 324, 336   2nd: 7, 91, 125, 154, 245, 296, 394, 395, 405

	O	M	R	W	O	M	R	W
Wall	34.1	10	72	5	29	6	75	1
O'Reilly	50	19	82	2	50.3	21	79	4
Ironmonger	20	6	50	1	57	21	87	3
Grimmett	28	6	94	2	35	9	74	1
McCabe	14	5	28	0	16	0	42	0
Bradman	14	5	28	0	4	0	25	1

Australia

Batsman	1st innings	R	2nd innings	R
Fingleton	c Ames b Allen	0	b Larwood	0
Woodfull	b Allen	22	not out	73
Bradman	c Allen b Larwood	8	c and b Verity	66
McCabe	c Jardine b Larwood	8	c Leyland b Allen	7
Ponsford	b Voce	85	c Jardine b Larwood	3
Richardson	b Allen	28	c Allen b Larwood	21
Oldfield	retired hurt	41	absent hurt	0
Grimmett	c Voce b Allen	10	b Allen	6
Wall	b Hammond	6	b Allen	0
O'Reilly	b Larwood	0	b Larwood	5
Ironmonger	not out	0	b Allen	0
Extras	Byes 2, lb 11, nb 1	14	Byes 4, lb 2, w 1, nb 5	12
Total		**222**		**193**

FOW 1st: 1, 18, 34, 51, 131, 194, 212, 222   2nd: 3, 12, 100, 116, 171, 183, 185, 192, 193

	O	M	R	W	O	M	R	W
Larwood	25	6	35	3	19	3	71	4
Allen	25	4	71	4	17.2	5	50	4
Hammond	17.4	4	30	1	9	3	27	0
Voce	14	5	21	1	4	1	7	0
Verity	16	7	51	0	20	12	26	1

Fourth Test, Brisbane - England won by 6 wickets
10, 11, 12, 13, 14, 16 February 1933   Umpires: G. Borwick and G.A. Hele

Australia

Woodfull		b Mitchell	67		c Hammond	b Mitchell	19
Richardson	st Ames	b Hammond	83		c Jardine	b Verity	32
Bradman		b Larwood	76		c Mitchell	b Larwood	24
McCabe	c Jardine	b Allen	20			b Verity	22
Ponsford		b Larwood	19		c Larwood	b Allen	0
Darling	c Ames	b Allen	17		run out		39
Bromley	c Verity	b Larwood	26		c Hammond	b Allen	7
Love	lbw	b Larwood	5		lbw	b Larwood	3
Wall	not out		6		c Jardine	b Allen	2
O'Reilly	c Hammond	b Larwood	17			b Larwood	4
Ironmonger	st Ames	b Hammond	8		not out		0
	Byes 5, lb 1, nb 1		7		Byes 13, lb 9, nb 1		23
		Total	340			Total	175

FOW 1st: 133, 200, 233, 264, 267, 293, 313, 317, 329   2nd: 46, 79, 81, 91, 136, 163, 169, 169, 171

	O	M	R	W	O	M	R	W
Larwood	31	7	101	4	17.3	3	49	5
Allen	24	4	83	2	17	3	44	5
Hammond	23	5	61	2	10	4	18	0
Mitchell	16	5	49	2	5	0	11	1
Verity	27	12	39	0	19	6	50	2

England

Jardine	c Love	b O'Reilly	46		lbw	b Ironmonger	24
Sutcliffe	lbw	b O'Reilly	86		c Darling	b Wall	2
Hammond		b McCabe	20		c Bromley	b Ironmonger	14
Wyatt	c Love	b Ironmonger	12				
Leyland	c Bradman	b O'Reilly	12		c McCabe	b O'Reilly	86
Ames	c Darling	b Ironmonger	17		not out		14
Allen	c Love	b Wall	13				
Paynter	c Richardson	b Ironmonger	83		not out		14
Larwood		b McCabe	23				
Verity	not out		23				
Mitchell	lbw	b O'Reilly	0				
	Byes 6, lb 12, nb 3		21		Byes 2, lb 4, nb 2		8
		Total	356			Total	162

FOW 1st: 114, 157, 165, 188, 198, 216, 225, 264, 356   2nd: 5, 78, 118, 158

	O	M	R	W	O	M	R	W
Wall	25	6	66	1	7	1	17	1
O'Reilly	67.4	27	120	4	50	11	65	1
Ironmonger	43	19	69	3	55	13	47	2
McCabe	25	7	40	2	7.4	2	25	0
Bromley	10	4	19	0	..	..	..	..
Bradman	7	1	17	0	..	..	..	..
Darling	2	0	4	0	..	..	..	..

Fifth Test, Sydney – England won by 8 wickets
23, 24, 25, 27, 28 February 1933　　Umpires: G. Borwick and G.A. Hele

Australia

Batsman		1st innings		2nd innings
Richardson	c Jardine b Larwood	0	c Allen b Larwood	0
Woodfull	b Larwood	14	b Allen	67
Bradman	b Larwood	48	b Verity	71
O'Brien	c Larwood b Voce	61	c Verity b Voce	5
McCabe	c Hammond b Verity	73	c Jardine b Voce	4
Darling	b Verity	85	c Wyatt b Verity	7
Oldfield	run out	52	c Wyatt b Verity	5
Lee	c Jardine b Verity	42	b Allen	15
O'Reilly	b Allen	19	b Verity	1
Alexander	not out	17	lbw b Verity	0
Ironmonger	b Larwood	1	not out	0
	Byes 13, lb 9, w 1	23	Byes 4, nb 3	7
	Total	435	Total	182

FOW 1st: 0, 59, 64, 163, 244, 328, 385, 414, 430　2nd: 0, 115, 135, 139, 148, 161, 177, 178, 178

	O	M	R	W	O	M	R	W
Larwood	32.2	10	98	4	11	0	44	1
Voce	24	3	80	1	10	0	54	2
Allen	25	1	128	1	11.4	2	54	2
Hammond	8	0	52	0	5	0	10	0
Verity	17	3	62	3	19	9	55	5
Wyatt	2	0	12	0	–	–	–	–

England

Batsman		1st innings		2nd innings
Sutcliffe	c Richardson b O'Reilly	56		
Jardine	c Oldfield b O'Reilly	18	c Richardson b Ironmonger	24
Hammond	lbw b Lee	101	not out	75
Larwood	c Ironmonger b Lee	98		
Leyland	run out	42	b Ironmonger	0
Wyatt	c Ironmonger b O'Reilly	51	not out	61
Ames	run out	4		
Paynter	b Lee	48		
Allen	c Bradman b Lee	9		
Verity	c Oldfield b Alexander	7		
Voce	not out	4		
	Byes 7, lb 7, nb 2	16	Byes 6, lb 1, nb 1	8
	Total	454	Total	168

FOW 1st: 51, 153, 245, 310, 330, 349, 374, 418, 434　2nd: 43, 45

	O	M	R	W	O	M	R	W
Alexander	35	1	129	1	11	2	25	0
McCabe	12	1	27	0	5	2	10	0
O'Reilly	45	7	100	3	15	5	32	0
Ironmonger	31	15	64	0	26	12	34	2
Lee	40.2	10	111	4	12.2	3	52	0
Darling	7	5	5	0	2	0	7	0
Bradman	1	0	4	0	–	–	–	–

Series Averages: England

Batting

Name	Inns	NO	HS	Runs	Avge
Paynter	5	2	83	184	61.33
Hammond	9	1	112	440	55.00
Sutcliffe	9	1	194	440	55.00
Wyatt	9	2	78	327	46.71
Pataudi	3	0	102	122	40.66
Leyland	9	0	86	306	34.00
Verity	5	1	45	114	28.50
Larwood	7	1	98	145	24.16
Allen	7	0	48	163	23.28
Jardine	9	0	56	199	22.11
Ames	8	1	69	113	16.14
Voce	6	2	8	29	7.21
Bowes	2	2	4*	4	–
Mitchell	1	0	0	0	–

Bowling

Name	O	M	Runs	Wkts	Avge
Larwood	220	42	644	33	19.51
Mitchell	21	5	60	3	20.00
Verity	135	54	271	11	24.65
Voce	133.3	23	407	15	27.13
Allen	170.6	29	593	21	28.23
Hammond	120.3	27	291	9	32.33
Bowes	25	2	70	1	70.00
Wyatt	2	0	12	0	–

Series Averages: Australia

Batting

Name	Inns	NO	HS	Runs	Avge
Bradman	8	1	103*	396	56.57
McCabe	10	1	187*	385	42.77
Darling	4	0	85	148	37.00
Woodfull	10	1	73*	305	33.88
Lee	2	0	42	57	28.50
Richardson	10	0	83	279	27.90
Oldfield	7	2	52	136	27.20
Fingleton	6	0	83	150	25.00
Ponsford	6	0	85	141	23.50
O'Brien	4	0	61	87	21.75
Nagel	2	1	21*	21	21.00
Alexander	2	1	17*	17	17.00
Bromley	2	0	26	33	16.50
Kippax	2	0	19	27	13.50
Grimmett	6	0	19	42	7.00
O'Reilly	10	0	19	61	6.10
Wall	8	1	20	42	6.00
Love	2	0	5	8	4.00
Ironmonger	8	5	8	13	2.60

Bowling

Name	O	M	Runs	Wkts	Avge
Wall	160.1	33	409	16	25.56
O'Reilly	383.4	144	724	27	26.81
Ironmonger	245.1	96	405	15	27.00
Lee	52.4	13	163	4	40.75
Bradman	12	1	44	1	44.00
Nagel	43.4	9	110	2	55.00
Grimmett	147	41	326	5	65.20
McCabe	92.5	17	215	3	71.66
Alexander	46	2	154	1	154.00
Kippax	2	1	3	0	–
Darling	11	5	14	0	–
Bromley	10	4	19	0	–

Catches taken by England
excludes wicket-keepers

Name	Tests	Other matches	Total
Verity	3	16	19
Jardine	9	7	16
Allen	7	7	14
Hammond	6	8	14
Mitchell	1	10	11
Wyatt	2	7	9
Brown	0	8	8
Voce	3	4	7
Pataudi	0	6	6
Ames	0	6	6
Sutcliffe	1	4	5
Paynter	0	5	5
Leyland	2	2	4
Larwood	2	1	3
Tate	0	3	3
Bowes	0	1	1
Totals:	36	95	131

Lightning Source UK Ltd.
Milton Keynes UK
25 August 2009

143083UK00002B/2/P